OPTIMAL

MONEY

FLOW

LAWRENCE C. MARSH

OPTIMAL

A New Vision of How a Dynamic-Growth

MONEY

Economy Can Work for Everyone

FLOW

AVILA
UNIVERSITY
PRESS

Published by Avila University Press
11901 Wornall Road
Kansas City, MO 64145

Copyright ©2020 Lawrence C. Marsh

All rights reserved.

Distributed by Greenleaf Book Group

For ordering information or special discounts for bulk purchases, please contact Greenleaf Book Group at PO Box 91869, Austin, TX 78709, 512.891.6100.

Design and composition by Greenleaf Book Group
Cover design by Greenleaf Book Group

Publisher's Cataloging-in-Publication data is available.

Print ISBN: 978-1-7342252-0-4

eBook ISBN: 978-1-7342252-1-1

Audiobook ISBN: 978-1-7342252-2-8

Part of the Tree Neutral® program, which offsets the number of trees consumed in the production and printing of this book by taking proactive steps, such as planting trees in direct proportion to the number of trees used: www.treeneutral.com

TreeNeutral®

Printed in the United States of America on acid-free paper

20 21 22 23 24 25   10 9 8 7 6 5 4 3 2 1

First Edition

I would especially like to thank Janet K. Marsh, Erik Tyler, Elizabeth Brown, and Jeffrey Curry for their perspective, insights, and guidance in the writing, editing, and publishing of this book.

CONTENTS

PREFACE

My wife and I had just gotten back from the bank. As we pulled into the garage, I saw some papers blowing around the front yard and told my wife I would go and get them. We left the garage door open as she swept the walk and I chased the papers.

We had seen the stranger in the alley behind our home earlier that day. But we didn't see him sneak into the garage, grab my wife's purse, and steal her cash.

The next day I saw him again. This time I followed him down the alley. When I caught up with him, I explained that anyone stealing small amounts of money here and there was making a mistake. I told him what he really needed was not money but money flow. These neighborhood families were making six-figure salaries, but he was just getting occasional crumbs. Fighting over the crumbs is no way to get rich, neither for an individual, nor for a country. I never saw him again. Perhaps he was afraid of getting caught or wanted to avoid another boring lecture.

Money flow is important in the international economy, in the domestic economy, and in state, city, and local economies, just as it is in our own family's economy. Too often we think of money as a static concept. We fight over the economic pie. But, in reality, money is a dynamic flow. Money flows through our economy just as blood flows through our body.

Our economic well-being and that of our fellow citizens is more closely defined by our money flow than by the amount of money we have at any particular time. Just as getting money flow right is important for us as individuals, it is also important for us at the local, state, national, and international levels.

Market efficiency requires that marginal benefits match marginal costs. College courses in introductory economics focus on the purest form of market equilibrium, where there are no externalities; no common property resources; no public goods; no fallacies of composition; no deviations from transparent, full-information, competitive markets; and where, at least on average, consumers behave as rational, independent decision makers. Traditional economic theory treats government as exogenous to the system with, at least in theory, no essential role to play other than to maintain the peace and enforce contracts.

Of all these sins of commission or omission, one of the worst is the fallacy of composition that confuses microeconomics with macroeconomics. Too often people make the mistake of assuming that individual-level microeconomic incentives can simply be aggregated to determine economy-wide macroeconomic effects. A simple example is what economists call the *paradox of thrift*, where everyone trying to save more during a recession (an example of microeconomic activity) leads to a reduction in total savings as the economy shrinks (a macroeconomic effect). In other words, more people trying to save more during a recession leads to a fall, rather than a rise, in total savings. Understanding microeconomic incentives does not automatically inform us about which macroeconomic policies will lead to efficient resource allocation.

Money flow dynamics are subject to the laws of mathematics. This is especially important for achieving economic stability and equilibrium. When you square a number between zero and one, it gets smaller. But squaring a number greater than one makes it bigger.[1] We have learned from *The Black Swan*[2] and other such analyses that the parameters that control our economy do not always stay between zero and one and, therefore, do not always move us toward convergent stability and equilibrium. Instead, our economy can be driven by contagion effects and other automatic processes toward divergent instability in the face of either irrational exuberance or a downward recessionary spiral.

George Cooper has proposed a wealth flow—or money flow—paradigm with government at the center of capitalism and the free enterprise system.[3] Cooper points out that before 1628, the medical profession mistakenly followed a blood flow paradigm (framework for thinking) that assumed that our blood originated in the liver and flowed outward where it evaporated at our extremities (fingers and toes). Previous economic paradigms have followed a similar path in assuming that government is, or at least should be, just an outside observer with no essential role to play in economic activity, when in reality, government is the heart of the free enterprise system, with money flowing in a circular loop.

The new money flow paradigm replaces the classical, neoclassical, Austrian, monetarist, and Keynesian schools of economic thought, which are all based on the old "exogenous" government paradigm and assume that government generally detracts from the efficient allocation of resources. In contrast, the money flow paradigm sees government as playing a key role in bringing about economic efficiency. There are many

---

1   More generally, squaring parameters that lie between minus one and plus one (the unit circle in multidimensional space) drives the effect toward zero, but squaring parameters that lie outside the unit circle drives it farther from zero.

2   Taleb, Nassim Nicholas. *The Black Swan: The Impact of the Highly Improbable*. New York: Random House, 2007.

3   Cooper, George. *Fixing Economics*. Hampshire: Harriman House Ltd., 2016.

circumstances where government corrects free market allocations and brings marginal benefits in line with marginal costs.

In an earlier book, Cooper rejected the efficient market hypothesis that is explicitly or implicitly endorsed by most of the previous paradigms.[4] Under his financial instability hypothesis, Cooper notes that while markets for goods and services generally operate efficiently, with negative feedback loops slowing demand as prices rise and increasing demand as prices fall, financial markets tend to do the opposite using positive feedback loops: rising prices increase demand, and falling prices drive investors to sell their shares and leave the market.

To fully understand the impact of economic policy, we must follow all the various paths that money takes in flowing through our economy with the different multiplier effects and different monetary velocities in each path. And we must consider the role government plays. The balanced budget multiplier only works if higher taxes are paid by those who spend less as a group on new products and services, and government expenditures go to those who spend more as a group in increasing the demand for goods and services. In other words, money is simply being transferred from a group of people with a low marginal propensity to consume goods and services to one with a high marginal propensity to consume. This enables the federal government to maintain a balanced budget and not add to our national debt while, at the same time, stimulating our economy to get out of a recession.

A contractionary policy could be devised to do the opposite when the economy is booming and inflation is getting out of hand. In that case, the money flow to investors (who will use it to expand our economy's productive capacity) should be increased while reducing the money flow

---

4   Cooper, George. *The Origin of Financial Crises*. New York: Vintage, 2008.

to consumers who are causing too much money to chase too few goods and services (which causes excessive inflation).

Money has a natural tendency to pile up at the top of the economic pyramid. Government plays an essential role in keeping money flowing back down to the middle and lower classes, who otherwise would be unable to buy back the goods and services they are producing. This is in sharp contrast to the traditional paradigms that have prevailed in economics for hundreds of years, which view government as an outside force whose interference is seen as alien to capitalism and free enterprise, and which must be kept to a minimum.

Under the old paradigms, when individuals or businesses spend money, they are seen as attempting to increase their utility or profits; but when government taxes and spends to benefit the community as a whole, the tax is seen as a waste of resources, disassociated from the corresponding public expenditure that increases public utility and improves the common good.

The fundamental flaw in the old paradigms is the failure to recognize that government plays a large and essential role in correcting capitalism's inherent distortions and defects. In a mistaken interpretation of Adam Smith's *The Wealth of Nations*,[5] a blind pursuit of one's own self-interest was thought to make everyone better off. Economists have carried out scientific experiments demonstrating that this is not the way people actually behave and that such self-interested behavior does not always make everyone better off. Yes, competition can work to provide high-quality products at low cost; but it can sometimes become distorted by a multitude of factors that can lead to an unhealthy, underperforming

---

5   Smith, Adam. *An Inquiry into the Nature and Causes of the Wealth of Nations*. London: Printed for Thomas Dobson, at the stone house in Second Street, 1789.

economy with inefficient resource allocation and extreme wealth and income inequality.

If I owned the only store and restaurant on a remote island, I would profit by paying my employees, local farmers, and fishermen well so that they could afford to come back again and again to buy goods at my store and eat at my restaurant. Good money flow would work to my advantage.[6] I would have a clear self-interest in maintaining money flow in my community. But if my restaurant is in a larger community, I can't directly generate more business for myself by paying my employees and suppliers more. The money I pay them gets dispersed out into the broader community. Our free enterprise system naturally leads to an ever-greater accumulation of wealth at the top of the economic pyramid that can only be alleviated by government intervention. The money flow paradigm takes into account the common property resource nature of our economy and proposes policies that redirect the money flow to restore efficient resource allocation and maximize our productive capacity.

Neoclassical economists assume that prices, wages, and interest rates will adjust automatically and relatively quickly to correct this problem. Keynesian economists and others recognize problems such as the liquidity trap, where the economy can sometimes get stuck and needs a little help from the government (fiscal or monetary stimulus) to get back on track.

Only the new money flow paradigm sees this as a permanent problem that is not going away. It will get worse until we finally change our

---

6   Until available resources are fully employed, the faster money turns over in a given time period, the more goods and services are produced and distributed. Everyone works more, and everyone gets more. Getting the money flow right is key to maintaining a healthy, dynamically growing economy to maximize the production and distribution of goods and services.

view and understand that the very nature of economics itself leads to a distorted money flow that requires a new mechanism (see "My America" prosperity accounts in chapter 3) to keep money flowing throughout the economy. Under the money flow paradigm, government must take up its role as the heart of the free enterprise system to keep money properly and adequately circulating to maintain full employment and stable prices.

What we have failed to recognize is that the broader economy is, by definition, a common property resource, because we all benefit from it, but as individuals we do not want to pay the taxes for the public investments needed to maintain it. When I was a child, everyone in our neighborhood burned their leaves by the side of the road in the fall. Any one family who stopped burning leaves did little to clear the air, as others continued to burn theirs. The only solution was for the town of Westfield to ban all leaf burning to clear the air, which was, by definition, a common property resource. Professors Elinor Ostrom and Oliver Williamson won the Nobel Prize in economics in 2009 for their work in explaining the role of common property resources in economics.[7] Just as we destroy value by overfishing a commonly owned lake until the fish are all gone, as individuals and businesses we fail to put enough money back into the economy to maintain an adequate money flow. We fail to invest in our future, like a farmer who does nothing in the spring in the hope that the crop will somehow seed, fertilize, and water itself. At a time when other countries throughout the world are investing a lot of money in their digital and physical infrastructure, in the education and health of their citizens, and in basic research for national defense, we are letting our lead in all these important areas slip away.

---

7   Ostrom, Elinor. *Governing the Commons*. Cambridge: Cambridge University Press, 1990. Williamson, Oliver. *The Mechanisms of Governance*. Oxford: Oxford University Press, 1996.

This raises some important questions. Why would a pharmaceutical company invest a lot of time and money into a breakthrough cancer drug if the potential medical benefit could be obtained from ingredients readily available to the average person, or if the return on its investment took too long to achieve? The answer: the company wouldn't bother. Therefore, why not consider funding medical and scientific research through the National Institutes of Health and the National Science Foundation, which provide financial support to university researchers who are more interested in enhancing their professional reputations than achieving monopoly profits?[8]

Do patents encourage innovation or suppress it? Has the "starve the beast" philosophy gone too far in shrinking government resources to the point where we are no longer able to compete in these vital areas? In clinging to the past and failing to invest in our future, are we transforming American exceptionalism from America first to America last? We need to answer these questions to achieve an optimal money flow in health, education, infrastructure, research, and in our economy overall.

During a recession, when demand is insufficient to ensure full employment, continuously falling prices do not generate more demand for goods and services, because people come to expect lower future prices and hold back on immediate expenditures in anticipation of even lower prices to come. Traditional static economic analysis misses this point. Only a truly dynamic analysis of how anticipated inflation affects money flow can fully incorporate this. Why pay a high price now if you see that prices are going down? Buying anything other than the bare essentials will make you a "loser" for paying too high a price for a good or service.

---

8   This contrasts with Paul Romer's endogenous growth theory that assumes new ideas are generally produced by the private sector in for-profit businesses.

As a medium of exchange, a unit of account, a store of value, and a method of deferred payment, money is retained rather than spent when consumers expect prices to continue falling. Stimulating the economy can only be achieved by getting money into the hands of people who will actually spend it right away on immediate necessities rather than hold off purchasing luxuries until prices stop falling precipitously. Slowly rising prices will encourage people to spend more money now to move the economy back toward full employment. However, monetary authorities must continuously monitor the money flow to keep inflation within a narrow target range. Left to its own devices, without government intervention, an overly stimulated economy will inherently and perversely generate faster and faster spending when excessive inflation drives consumers to anticipate higher and higher prices.

Taxation is not an interference with an otherwise efficiently operating economy; rather, government taxation and expenditures are essential components of the money flow needed to maintain and adequately grow a healthy economy. A properly designed fiscal policy can contribute to economic growth with a balanced budget multiplier by taxing those with a low marginal propensity to consume and getting money flowing by making appropriate investments, such as in infrastructure, basic research, education, and health. Government taxation and expenditures overcome the common property resource problem by providing the necessary investments in the community. Properly designed fiscal policy can improve rather than detract from efficient resource allocation.

Local, state, national, and international economies can interact to achieve an optimal money flow to maximize efficient resource allocation. By establishing an optimal money flow, we can maintain a healthy economy by improving the efficiency of our economy, reinvigorating productivity, and enhancing our lives.

CHAPTER 1

INTRODUCTION
TO THIS BOOK

This book introduces the money flow paradigm that explains the dynamic, interdependent nature of our economy and the causes of the tendency toward extreme income and wealth inequality that inherently lead to inefficient resource allocation and instability. It emphasizes how 21st-century technology, greatly enhanced by the internet, has produced an underlying transformation from a variable-cost economy—where each additional unit of output costs a great deal to produce—to a fixed-cost economy—where the initial setup costs are quite high, but each additional unit of output (e.g., another Facebook user account) requires very little additional cost—that has shifted the money flow from labor to capital over time. Moreover, failure to invest in our economy for the long run will leave us behind the world in general, and China in particular, as we rapidly advance into the 21st century. Education, basic research, and infrastructure require substantial investments.

Recognizing differences in the marginal propensity to consume by income and wealth is central to effective economic policy in dampening our economy's boom and bust cycle. Traditional economics assumes rational, independent decision makers and emphasizes a (long-run) tendency toward equilibrium while ignoring contagion effects that reinforce the centrifugal forces driving upward toward irrational exuberance or spiraling downward toward recession. In contrast to the classical, neoclassical, monetarist, and Keynesian paradigms, the new government-centered money flow paradigm views such forces as a natural part of the economic system and not as some exogenous shock to the system. Such perverse forces are just as central to and inherent in the free market system as its helpful, self-correcting forces and should be recognized as such.

It is important to recognize that each human being has both an *individual identity* and a *collective identity*. We are constantly being torn between these two identities. Think of the basketball player who must choose between self-promotion by taking the long shot or passing to a teammate much closer to the basket. Collectively we are most often represented according to where we live. Our neighborhood association, our city, our county, our state, and our country, as well as the world as a whole, are there to represent our collective identity to some degree or another. All of our identities—individual and collective—play a role in economics.

Treating government as an outside, alien force is naïve at best. Recognizing the existence of an implicit national social welfare function would enable us to rewrite economics textbooks to recognize the common-property nature of our economy and treat government as a legitimate player—alongside individual persons and businesses. Under the law, the power of government is limited, just as the power of businesses over their employees is also limited. Treating government as endogenous (within the system) rather than exogenous (outside the system) is more realistic and provides a much better understanding of how our economic system actually operates.

International trade has an ever-greater impact on our economy as the global supply chain has become increasingly complicated and interdependent. Productivity spillover effects and the law of comparative advantage play an important role in our national money flow and in our economic well-being. The international arena is another realm where the "win-win" strategy wins and the "I-win-you-lose" strategy loses. Countries that build bridges to reach out and help one another will have better money flow and healthier economies than those who wall off their neighbors to go it alone.

The special interests that often control our governmental policies and legislation frequently promote the idea that there are a fixed number of jobs in this world. But what they are really worried about is that low unemployment means having to pay higher wages, which, in turn, may bring on an inflation in prices that would undermine the real value of their enormous accumulated wealth.

Nothing limits the quantity and quality of jobs more than a government policy designed to protect special interests at the expense of everyone else. In truth, the economy would be better off with a little inflation, because it enables a faster transition from old, out-of-date technologies to new, up-to-date technologies. The current Federal Reserve target of 2 percent inflation was chosen with this in mind.

The special interest "starve-the-beast" strategies at best inhibit and at worst block our government's efforts to maintain a stable and healthy economy for everyone. We need to disentangle our economic policies from the stranglehold of politics. This means protecting our economy from distorted money flow policies that restrict economic growth and produce large unsustainable deficits.

A major problem with monetary policy is the long time lag between when the Federal Reserve takes action and when the full impact of that action is felt by the economy. The Fed may hit the brakes too hard by raising interest rates in response to inflation, resulting in an unneces-sary recession. In response to a recession, the Fed may find that releas-ing money into the financial markets by buying Treasury securities is as ineffective as "pushing on a string." The Fed's large purchases of Treasury securities primarily produce a stock market bubble, with a relatively small, lagged effect on consumer demand, which constitutes about 70 percent of the economy. Clearly, a more efficient method of controlling money flow is needed.

In its responsibility for carrying out monetary policy, the Fed needs direct and immediate control of the level of consumer demand for goods and services. All banks already have accounts (directly or indirectly) with the Federal Reserve System. Every person with a Social Security number should be issued a Federal Reserve Bank account that they could access with their smartphone.[1]

By establishing individual accounts for every person with a Social Security number, the Fed would be able to expand (by injecting money) and contract (by raising account interest rates) the money supply directly, having an immediate impact on the money flow throughout the economy, without needing to raise or lower taxes or increase the national debt, all the while maintaining a tight grip on any chance of excessive inflation.[2]

This direct method of injecting money into the economy requires considerably fewer dollars and has a quicker and more substantial impact

---

1   For those younger than 18 years old, the accounts could be used to provide a basic uni-versal income or create "baby bonds," as proposed by Senator Cory Booker and a number of economists.

2   A voluntary public option for Federal Reserve individual accounts was proposed by Morgan Ricks, John Crawford, and Lev Menand in "A Public Option for Bank Accounts (Or Central Banking for All)," Vanderbilt Law Research Paper 18–33; UC Hastings Research Paper No. 287. June 6, 2018.

on consumer demand than buying Treasury securities in the New York financial markets. It offers much more "bang for the buck."

Chapter 2 ("History of Money Flow") describes how economic power evolved from primitive times through the Industrial Revolution and the rise of capitalism. It discusses how John Locke's concept of private property as a function of sweat equity was undermined by the separation of labor from capital. Moreover, money flow was diverted from labor to capital as technological advances have reduced variable costs (labor) relative to fixed costs (capital), leading to ever-greater extremes in income and wealth inequality.

Chapter 3 ("Money Flow Dynamics") reviews the creation and use of money and the key role it plays in determining both employment and inflation in a dynamic economy. Static analysis focuses on fighting over a fixed pie following an I-win-you-lose strategy, while dynamic analysis follows a win-win strategy where a dynamic money flow leads to a healthy, rapidly growing economy that benefits everyone.

Chapter 4 ("Money Flow Coopetition") examines money flow between businesses, as well as that between businesses and government. The traditional assumption in economics of rational, independent decision makers is shown to be misleading. Mistakes include applying microeconomic conclusions to macroeconomics and treating government as exogenous to the economic system.

Chapter 5 ("Government") concerns the role of government in using money flow to achieve efficient resource allocation. Market failures include positive externalities, negative externalities, common property resources, public goods, and asymmetric information, as well as monopolies, oligopolies, monopsonies, and oligopsonies. Each requires public or private collective adjustments to properly match marginal benefits to marginal costs.

Chapter 6 ("Distorted Money Flow") explores how the American tradition of *noblesse oblige* inspired by the French Revolution was replaced by the *nouveau riche* with a winner-take-all strategy that led to maximizing the wealth of special interests. The Supreme Court's *Citizens United* decision certified "pay-to-play" through tax loopholes, lower taxation on earnings from capital than from labor, and a host of other regulatory and spending adjustments favoring the special interests. As a result, large corporations and special interests often pay little or no taxes, while small businesses and middle-class taxpayers pay substantially more.

Chapter 7 (**"Macroeconomic Policy"**) promotes fiscally prudent money flow, which would keep the economy on an even keel to avoid extreme oscillations from high unemployment to high inflation. The analysis covers the national debt, automatic stabilizers, Federal Reserve policy, the liquidity trap, and a proposal for the creation of individual "My America" Federal Reserve accounts for everyone over 18 who has a Social Security number.

Chapter 8 (**"International Money"**) examines the impact of international trade on jobs, prices, competition, and investment returns. The lump of labor fallacy is explained, and alternative job creation policies are discussed. Population growth, education, and technology play key roles in affecting the money flow both within and between nations. Foreign aid is used to promote exports. Energy, natural resources, and the *Dutch disease* all play important parts in international money flow.

Chapter 9 (**"Summary"**) focuses and reiterates the discussion and analyses from all the previous chapters.

CHAPTER 2

HISTORY OF MONEY FLOW: TECHNOLOGY FAVORS FIXED COSTS AND LABOR LOSES OUT

I n prehistoric times the freedom of cave dwellers depended on physical strength. If you had a chicken, the big guy was free to take your chicken. If you had a pear tree, the big guy was free to take your pears. Today our brains are still wired to submit to the winner. Our submission to authority and acquiescence to the winner-take-all outcome reasserts itself again and again throughout our lives.[3] A single leader has traditionally dominated, starting in primitive times with a large, powerful male.

---

3   This effect is evident in our adulation of leaders in sports and entertainment. See Rosen, Sherwin. "The Economics of Superstars." *The American Economic Review*, Vol. 71, No. 5 (December 1981): 845–858.

In most societies the tribal leader, the chief, the king, the pharaoh, the emperor, or the tsar controlled everything. You were free to do as you were told, but not free to do what you wanted.

The Greeks were the first civilization in recorded history to try a version of democracy. Northern Europeans didn't crack the authoritarian ceiling until the Magna Carta in 1215. The American and French Revolutions overthrew the king's rule, but we still have a tendency to revert back to a system of political and economic autocracy. As in Russia today, an autocratic leader can divert the money flow to benefit special interests who use their power and money to control the political system and the economy. And yet such a leader can still be popular with a majority of citizens.

People can be kept under control with nice-sounding slogans and threats of foreign domination, as occurs in North Korea, where very little money trickles down to the common person. People can be deceived into accepting such a system, because they do not really understand how money flow works to establish and maintain a healthy economy.

ORIGINS OF MONEY FLOW

Originally, both European and Native American cultures viewed land as belonging to God or the divine spirits. People could occupy land, but not own it. Eventually kings, pharaohs, emperors, and tsars were said to have been granted dominion over the land by God. You could not hunt deer in the forest or take fish from a stream without permission from the king. Rulers could then allocate lands for the nobility. For example, in Colonial America, King George allocated land in New Jersey to early settlers under the Elizabethtown Grant. Even in early years of the United States of America, only land-owning Caucasian men could vote, while non-Caucasians, women, and the landless had no say in government.

The need to enclose land for agriculture and to motivate people to work the land required the creation of a more broadly based concept of private property.

Before the Industrial Revolution, John Locke (1632–1704) introduced the basic principle establishing the right to own private property.[4] He argued that people owned their own labor, and that by putting their labor into the land, they created their right of land ownership or private property. In the second part of his *Two Treatises of Government* (1689), Locke essentially argued that by working the land and other artifacts of the natural world, a person could establish ownership of property by what today might be called sweat equity. Initially this logically established the foundation for ownership in farming and the craft trades. The peasants worked hard on the land they now owned but still had to pay royalties to the king and nobility.

This concept worked well at first when craftsmen and craftswomen created and used their own tools. But the link between sweat equity and capital broke down when capital investment became too large for a single worker or group of workers to manage. For large capital investments, members of the nobility with greater command of resources would step in to make the necessary investment in a water mill for power or machinery in a factory. As a result, the broken link between sweat equity and the ownership of capital (e.g., machines) is systematically and inevitably causing more and more money to flow to the owners of capital and relatively less money to flow to workers.

Workers were no longer entitled to the fruits of their labor. No matter how long and how hard they worked with a machine, they failed to gain any ownership over that machine. They could imbue their labor into the machine they were working or the truck they were driving for

---

4   Locke, John. *Two Treatises of Government.* London: Awnsham Churchill, 1689.

their entire career of many, many years, but their autonomy and rights, as defined by Robert Nozick in his book *Anarchy, State, and Utopia*, were not respected.[5] They were denied the fruits of their labor just as surely as if taxed away by the state. Yes, they chose their employer, just as they chose what country, county, state, or locality to live in, but that does not justify breaking the link between sweat equity and capital.

To be fair, some companies recognize that the workers, as well as the original investors, have a legitimate claim on capital as it is used by the workers over time. Yet many companies ignore the workers' right of autonomy over the fruits of their labor and sweat equity and give all of the return on capital to the original investors, who over time add nothing more as they reap the rewards of other people's labor. We talk of the importance of incentives, but where is the incentive for workers to work hard for a company that denies their right to earn capital from sweat equity? All the return on capital is given to the original investors, whose only incentive is to spend their days watching the stock ticker as their money grows without any additional effort on their part.

Throughout most of human history, economic change has proceeded slowly. The invention of the wheel, the development of human language, and the establishment of agriculture were separated by long periods of little or no change. If you wanted to plant another row of corn, you found a big stick and worked up the soil. Labor was in great demand and capital was almost nonexistent. Most costs were variable costs, which were dominated by labor. Fixed costs representing capital were usually relatively small. Eventually, if you could afford it, you bought or borrowed a horse or mule to pull the plow. But, generally, more corn output meant a lot more labor input.

---

5   Nozick, Robert. *Anarchy, State, and Utopia*. New York: Basic Books, 1974.

ADAM SMITH CONCERNED ABOUT WEALTH DISTRIBUTION

This was the world that Adam Smith (1723–1790) faced when he wrote his books *The Theory of Moral Sentiments*[6] and *The Wealth of Nations*.[7] Smith explained how free enterprise in a competitive environment can improve the economic well-being of the nation as a whole. Businesses compete to provide the nation with the best-quality products at the lowest possible prices.[8] Smith implicitly assumed competitive markets where full information was readily available to all market participants. He did *not* "advocate unbridled greed and selfishness in the name of allowing the invisible hand of the market to work its magic."[9] Instead, he advocated for the poor and felt that too much attention was given to the rich. Smith noted that people like to think about happy conditions and not sad conditions, so they look to the rich, rather than the poor, for inspiration.

He saw that specialization and division of labor increased productivity but was concerned that it would go too far and leave workers with merely mechanical jobs where they had no sense of self-worth. Smith seemed to anticipate the production line and the robotic role that people would later play in the Industrial Revolution.

He did not advocate laissez-faire and capitalism. While he saw that

6   Smith, Adam. *The Theory of Moral Sentiments*. Edinburgh: Andrew Millar, in the Strand; and Alexander Kincaid and J. Bell, 1759.

7   Smith, Adam. *An Inquiry into the Nature and Causes of the Wealth of Nations*. London: W. Strahan and T. Cadell, 1776.

8   A more comprehensive summary of Smith's book can be found at https://en.wikipedia. org/wiki/The_Wealth_of_Nations.

9   See article by Dennis C. Rasmussen in the June 9, 2016, issue of *The Atlantic* at https://www.theatlantic.com/business/archive/2016/06/ the-problem-with-inequality-according-to-adam-smith/486071/.

the invisible hand was increasing output and productivity, he was concerned about the plight of the poor in society.

TWO INVISIBLE HANDS

The invisible hand that Adam Smith discovered was one of two invisible hands. Smith's invisible hand was the left invisible hand that serves *economic efficiency* by turning entrepreneurial self-interest into better-quality products at lower prices through competition. At the same time, the right invisible hand serves *economic power* in attempting to achieve market domination with barriers to entry and the acquisition of rivals. These two invisible hands are in constant struggle with each other. When the right invisible hand dominates, economic inefficiency and economic inequality can become extreme. This bad invisible hand must be constrained through regulation and globalization to ensure fair play and adequate competition. History is the story of this constant struggle between these two invisible hands.

SWEAT EQUITY TO CAPITAL LINK BROKEN

At the beginning of economic time, variable costs dominated fixed costs in the absence of any significant capital investments. Initiative, hard work, and enterprise paid off in ownership of your physical capital. If you made an arrowhead, it was your arrowhead. If you made a cutting tool, it was your cutting tool. Workers owned their own capital. The concept of private property was then extended to other physical and intellectual products. In the 19th century, the Industrial Revolution began an acceleration in economic development that has changed the very essence of the economic problem. The sweat equity path to ownership broke down with the advent of a more remote form of capitalism.

Money came into existence when bartering became too complicated and inefficient. Money made the transfer of property easier. But money was essentially just a promise to pay. Under the gold standard, all money was backed by gold. Later, when the government levied a substantial amount of taxes, the value of money was in part based on the need to pay your taxes with money.

The money flow debate began with the need to decide how much money the government should issue. But how the money flows through the economy depends upon all the fine print in the laws and regulations. Tax loopholes and incentives have unintended consequences that can alter the money flow.[10]

At one point in the 19th century, Argentina and the United States were at roughly the same stage of development and had somewhat comparable natural resources at their disposal. The United States looked westward to the Great Plains and Rocky Mountains while Argentina looked toward the broad fertile Pampas grasslands and the Andes Mountains. But their economic policies followed distinctly separate paths. In Argentina the land on the western frontier was allocated to the elite. Workers could farm the land under the tutelage of the elite, but the chances of their gaining ownership of any parcel of land were remote at best. This followed the tradition of the king awarding land

---

10   Too often we ignore the central role of government in determining money flow in our economy. We naïvely follow the golden path to the Emerald City and ignore the wizard behind the curtain who is pulling all the strings that determine how money flows to each and every one of us. Simplifying the tax code was supposed to replace the system of tax loopholes with a lower overall corporate tax rate. The 2017 tax law passed by Congress and signed into law by the president failed to remove the vast majority of tax loopholes and instead allowed corporations to combine their array of tax loopholes with the lower corporate tax rate, thus eliminating or at least dramatically reducing their corporate tax liability.

to aristocrats in Colonial America. In Argentina, Locke's link between sweat equity and ownership was broken.

However, in the United States, especially after the Civil War, the prospects of acquiring "forty acres and a mule" drove Americans westward.[11] A Union soldier who died in battle was said to have "bought the farm," as his descendants were awarded sufficient funds to pay off a modest mortgage as compensation for that soldier paying the ultimate price in service to his country. Money flowed to those who successfully worked the land. It was that money flow that ultimately enabled the United States to develop much more rapidly than Argentina, which remained dominated by elites for a much longer period.

As the Industrial Revolution proceeded, John Locke's original concept of private property broke down. A craft worker had indeed established ownership over his or her tools of trade in the early years. But soon the size and expense of industrial equipment, such as a lathe or water wheel, became too large for the individual worker to acquire through sweat equity. Only persons with sufficient capital could afford to acquire the industrial equipment that was then used by workers who were generally denied equity for their labor. Instead of motivating workers by enabling them to share in the risk-reward enterprise, workers were off-loaded to a separate labor track with a much lower return for their effort.

---

11 "Forty acres and a mule" refers to a proposal made by Union General William Tecumseh Sherman on January 16, 1865, for formerly enslaved African American farmers.

THE DEBT-DEFLATION CYCLE EMERGES

Once the link between sweat equity and capital was broken, money flowed more and more to capital. Workers had to go into debt to afford to buy back the goods and services they were producing, as capitalists accumulated enormous wealth in the late 19th and early 20th centuries. Occasionally government stepped in to break up monopolies and protect worker unions to counter excessive corporate power. Money flow became erratic as rapid economic expansions were followed by economic panics or, in modern parlance, recessions. Initially Irving Fisher came to appreciate this problem from his personal experience in the Great Depression of the 1930s. In 1933, Fisher described the pattern of debt inflation (as individuals and businesses got overextended by borrowing beyond their means), followed by debt deflation (as the bubble burst with a torrent of mortgage defaults and bankruptcies).[12] Fisher's key argument is that these debt cycles are inherent in our free enterprise system, with the buildup of excessive debt ultimately leading to a collapse in the debt bubble as entities reach a tipping point.[13]

Fisher used the analogy of a ship that ordinarily can rock from side to side and return to an upright position or equilibrium, unless it is subject to particularly strong wind and waves. According to Fisher, at some point, if wind and waves reach the tipping point and nothing is done to stabilize the ship, it capsizes.

But Fisher argues that the bursting of the debt bubble by itself is not sufficient to bring down the economy as a whole. Rather, it is the drop in prices or deflation that naturally follows the bursting of the debt bubble,

---

12 Fisher, Irving. "The Debt-Deflation Theory of Great Depressions." *Econometrica*, Vol. 1, No. 4 (October 1933): 337–357.

13 For an excellent discussion and explanation of our debt cycles, see Dalio, Ray. *Principles for Navigating BIG DEBT CRISES.* Westport, CT: Bridgewater Associates, LLP, 2018.

along with a slowing down in the velocity of circulation of money that produces a downward spiral toward recession or depression. Fisher said, "It would be as silly and immoral to 'let nature take her course' as for a physician to neglect a case of pneumonia." Fisher concluded that the federal government must step in to prevent deflation and the ultimate collapse of the economy.[14]

Zanny Minton Beddoes and her colleagues at *The Economist* have provided a concise and well-written analysis of the debt-deflation cycle and how, starting in the mid-1980s, the "Great Moderation" was maintained by central banks by adjusting short-term interest rates. But the global financial crisis of 2007–2008 revealed a deeper and inherently more difficult money flow problem.[15]

Hyman Minsky developed an elaborate theory explaining how economic stability led businesses and individuals to become overconfident, which, in turn, ultimately led to instability and economic collapse. From time to time the economy becomes naturally overextended with a growing debt bubble as consumers and businesses take on more and more debt. The image that emerges is Wile E. Coyote continuing to walk off the edge of the cliff into thin air until finally he sees that there is nothing supporting him. He then falls precipitously.[16]

While cycles in the stock market might be driven by "Minsky moments," the real economy is occasionally disrupted by technology

---

14   This is in sharp contrast to the Austrian paradigm, which argues for austerity in letting the economy contract and prices fall (especially wages) following Schumpeter's *Creative Destruction*. Instead of righting the ship, they would let it capsize.

15   Beddoes, Zanny Minton, et al. *Debts, Deficits and Dilemmas*. London: Profile Books, Ltd., 2014.

16   Minsky, Hyman P. *Stabilizing an Unstable Economy*. New Haven, CT: Yale University Press, 1986.

shocks. Randall Wright[17] and others have explained real business cycles in terms of abrupt changes in technology. Automation in manufacturing, such as in automobile production, has dramatically and abruptly reduced the demand for labor. Another major business cycle may be forthcoming due to a combination of autonomous vehicles and artificial intelligence algorithms replacing large numbers of workers.

Moreover, the delinking of labor from capital will eventually undermine worker motivation and productivity and slow down economic growth in the advanced economies of the world. The combination of slow growth and high expectations will inevitably lead to more "Minsky moments," where the private debt builds up and creates financial instability. This financial instability often results in a stock market correction and a dramatic drop in output and employment. This cycle has repeated itself again and again throughout US history.

MONEY FLOW SHIFTS FROM VARIABLE COSTS TO FIXED COSTS

Early settlers in the United States had only their bare hands and a few simple tools to farm the land. If they wanted to plant another row of corn, they had to take a shovel and work up the soil by hand. Most of the input into corn production was in the form of variable costs, which vary with the amount of output (in this case bushels of corn) being produced. In addition to seed and fertilizer, variable costs include lots of farmer labor hours of work. Over time the costs shifted to investments in farm equipment, which are fixed costs because the farm equipment has to be

---

17   Wright, Randall. "On the Future of Macro: A New Monetarist Perspective." *Oxford Review of Economic Policy*, Vol. 34, Nos. 1–2 (2018): 107–131.

paid for regardless of the level of corn output. If corn production drops to zero, the cost of seed, fertilizer, and labor hours drops to zero, but the fixed cost of the farm equipment still has to be paid.

Today, a farmer can sit in the farmhouse and monitor her self-driving plow at her computer—a plow that uses GPS to follow the correct path, all while measuring soil nutrient content and dispensing fertilizer as needed. The variable costs in the form of labor have been largely replaced with the fixed costs of creating the self-driving plow and all of the technology it uses in producing the corn crop.

Throughout the history of the United States, productivity has grown enormously while the money previously flowing to labor has shifted to capital. A similar story can be told in automobile production where fixed costs in the form of robotic equipment and technology have come to replace variable labor costs in the form of work hours and, ultimately, jobs. In addition to disrupting the vehicle manufacturing industry, in the coming decade self-driving trucks will replace millions of truck drivers on our roads. On the internet, almost all of the money flow goes to the fixed costs of setting up the website, with virtually no variable costs associated with adding an additional user to the site or with that user using the site.

In other words, using a website, which represents the fixed cost of capital investment, usually does not require interacting with a website worker, who represents the variable cost of labor. Even brick-and-mortar stores make ever-greater use of self-service and self-checkout, relying more and more on fixed-cost capital investment and less and less on store employees, who represent variable labor costs. Increasingly, capital is winning at the expense of labor. Replacing labor hours with fixed capital equipment reduces the money flowing to labor and increases the money flowing to capital investment. As technology advances, capital wins and labor loses.

The shift from an economy dominated by variable costs to one dominated by fixed costs was slow at first. In the 20th century, most machinery still required labor to operate it. At that time the exploration, development, and extraction of natural resources took a great deal of labor. In manufacturing, labor played a major role and a significant part of the cost of products and services. Sometimes this shift from labor meant a shift to self-service, in which the customer provided the labor. For example, self-service gasoline stations emerged late in the century, as did self-service checkout in retail stores.

In the 21st century, as the shift toward automation continues, the role of fixed costs has increased dramatically. Giant earth-moving equipment is used to extract coal by removing mountaintops rather than sending large numbers of miners underground. Automobile factories employ armies of robots in "lights-out" manufacturing where humans are relegated to much less labor-intensive roles, such as supervision and maintenance, while production continues on through the night in the dark. In recent decades, interstate highways, the internet, and globalization have enabled capital to become much more mobile than ever before. Money moves around the planet at the click of a mouse or a tap on a screen, whereas people are often reluctant to move from their home region to another region or country with a different culture and language.

Politicians railed against foreigners who were "taking our jobs" when, in reality, those jobs were destined for automation anyway. Even globalized jobs in low-wage markets will be overcome by the relentless march of technological progress. Wages have already risen sufficiently in Chinese factories to spur factory owners to consider saving money on labor by replacing it with capital, in the form of greater automation.

In the end, it is technology and not globalization that challenges our economic system. The stability of this system is at risk if we don't fully understand the impact of technology on money flow and fail to replace economic policy based on political interests with one centered on empirical, scientific evidence and innovative artificial intelligence methods of analysis.

Blaming the foreigners might make for good sound bites at political rallies, but it does nothing to help solve the real problem that is looming before us. The way we transfer goods across the country is a case in point. There are 3.5 million licensed professional truck drivers who will be losing their jobs before long. At first it will just be a small convoy of three or four driverless trucks, all automated except for one backup driver in the lead truck. After covering hundreds of miles on the highways, they will finally reach a truck stop near their final destination, where they will pick up local drivers for the short remaining trips. But even that part will ultimately be taken over by automation. Another million drivers will serve as local around-town drivers, such as local bus drivers, taxi drivers, and pizza delivery drivers. Sometime within the next ten years, many of them will begin to be replaced. Driverless trucks with vending machines will begin appearing at work sites and sports events. Automated drones will drop packages into home delivery boxes or down home delivery chutes.

As IBM's Deep Blue beat the established chess champions, Watson beat the best *Jeopardy!* contestants, and DeepMind's AlphaGo beat the best Go champions, the shift to physical and mental automation has picked up speed. IBM has recently announced major advances in quantum computing, which will enable computers to solve heretofore impossibly complex problems. Nor are changes limited to computer labs. Even in medicine, physicians will more and more depend on computer algorithms for diagnoses, recommended protocols, and prognoses.

The theme of the 20th century was mass production and one size fits all. The theme of the 21st century has become diversity and the uniqueness of the individual. This focus on uniqueness has required more complicated algorithms in almost every realm—from targeted advertising to individualized teaching and learning. The ever-increasing demands for mental skills have required even greater automation. In our digital life, variable costs have fallen dramatically as the cost of adding another user to Facebook is essentially zero. Jeremy Rifkin has astutely labeled this the "zero marginal cost society."[18]

SUMMARY, OVERVIEW, AND TRANSITION

This chapter has reviewed the history of how money, which originally flowed primarily to labor, has shifted over time to flow more and more to capital. The battle between labor and capital continues, with more education designed to enhance the power of labor, which economists call human capital[19] (i.e., labor enhanced through education), followed by greater application of artificial intelligence that improves robotics and adds to the power of capital.

While the benefits of additional education are diminished over time, the debt bubble grows as the middle class falls deeper and deeper into debt; this happens as those who derive their incomes from labor try to compete with those who derive their incomes from capital. Meanwhile, the continual decline of variable costs keeps labor at a disadvantage as the growing shift to fixed costs directs more and more money to capital. The continual buildup of debt for labor and massive savings for capital creates economic

continued

18   Rifkin, Jeremy. *The Zero Marginal Cost Society*. New York: St. Martin's Press, 2014.

19   Becker, Gary. *Human Capital: A Theoretical and Empirical Analysis, with Special Reference to Education*. Chicago: University of Chicago Press, 1964.

instability with simultaneous consumer debt bubbles and investor stock market bubbles.

The next chapter will explore the broader context of the role of money in our overall economy. It will discuss the common property resource nature of our overall economy, which prevents unassisted free enterprise from maintaining a proper money flow. A common property resource is a shared community resource, such as a publicly owned lake, the air we breathe, or the total demand for goods and services. Just as people may benefit as individuals from overfishing a lake, polluting the air, or decreasing their demand for goods and services during a recession, society as a whole would benefit from less excessive fishing and polluting, and from increasing consumer demand during economic downturns. The money flow paradigm presents government as the essential component in maintaining a healthy money flow in overcoming the common property resource problem and the natural booms and busts inherent in the free market system.

As George Cooper has made abundantly clear, the free market works great in nonfinancial markets with the buying and selling of consumer products and services, but it fails miserably in financial markets in the buying and selling of stocks, bonds, and a host of financial derivatives with perverse tendencies toward instability and disequilibrium. Under the money flow paradigm, the government takes direct control of the overall money flow as the key to maintaining a stable and healthy free market economy.

CHAPTER 3

MONEY FLOW DYNAMICS: AS BLOOD FLOWS THROUGH THE BODY

As a medium of exchange, money is worthless if there is no exchange. As a store of value, money can sit idle for hours, days, weeks, and years. Money flow can reflect the flow of newly produced products and services, or the exchange of existing items of value (e.g., rare paintings, exclusive real estate, expensive jewelry, or stocks and bonds).[20]

Money flow is international, national, regional, local, and personal. A healthy economy requires a healthy flow of money. In a stagnant

---

20 Working- and middle-class people have a higher marginal propensity to consume, so they are more likely to use any additional income to purchase services and new products, while wealthy people tend to save any additional money and invest it in equities or other existing items of value. Consequently, money received by working- or middle-class families is more likely to stimulate production and increase demand for services than that received by rich people.

economy, money does not flow adequately. In an inflationary economy, too much money is moving too fast for the economy to keep up.

Money flows through the economy as blood flows through the body. If money does not reach into all corners of the economy, it can pile up in some places (as fluids build up in congestive heart failure) and fail to reach other places, resulting in stagflation, reflecting an unbalanced money flow. In theory, such distortions should quickly disappear, but natural market forces can prevent a quick and full recovery. In reality, the economy can get caught in a liquidity trap with interest rates close to zero in real terms, which can keep unemployment high when money flow is inadequate to increase demand for goods and services sufficiently to achieve full capacity utilization.

THE QUANTITY AND QUALITY OF MONEY

People think of money as coins and currency. There is a lot more to it than that. Economists define money in various ways, depending upon how easy it is to convert to a form that is easy to spend.

Money is produced by the banking system. Paper money originated as IOUs issued by banks. Under the Federal Reserve Act of 1913, large banks were brought together to control the money supply. Currently, the money supply is controlled by the Federal Reserve System through its open market operations, as well as through the federal discount rate, the reserve requirements, and other regulatory means.

Money can be physical or digital. It can be backed by something of physical value, or backed by nothing but its own scarcity, as Bitcoin, Ether, Ripple, Litecoin, Libra, and other cryptocurrencies have clearly demonstrated. The idea that a country issuing currency is, in effect, issuing IOUs that must someday be paid off in gold or some other precious metal is misleading. Obviously, the cryptocurrency companies Bitcoin,

Ethereum, Ripple, Litecoin, and Facebook are offering currencies that, like gold, are just rare and hard to mine. But that fact has not undermined the acceptance of these new forms of currency.

Definitions of money range from very liquid to not so liquid. The M1 definition of money is the most liquid. M1 is defined as coins, currency, and checking account balances. It can be used directly without having to convert it to another form. The M2 definition includes M1 but adds savings account balances.

Creating money is easy for a bank. First, you deposit money in your bank account. Then, someone comes to the bank and arranges for a loan. Once the loan document is signed, the bank adds money to the borrower's bank account. Where does the bank get the money to loan out? It takes it from your bank account. Since you and the borrower are acting as if you both had immediate access to the same money, the bank has created money by the amount of the loan. Your bank has added to the money supply. Of course, it cannot do that with all of the money it receives, because it is required by law to keep some money in reserve.

Also, note that the Federal Reserve can counter any money supply changes by banks through the buying and selling of Treasury bills by the Federal Reserve Bank of New York in its open market operations. Ultimately, the Federal Reserve controls the money supply on a day-to-day basis in this way to keep interest rates on federal funds within a narrow range.

The Federal Deposit Insurance Corporation (FDIC) guarantees the dollar amounts of your deposits up to a set maximum but does not guarantee how much a dollar is worth in the economy. If inflation kicks in, the value of your money will decline. The value of money used to be guaranteed in terms of ounces of gold. Now there is no gold backing up our money. Without a guarantee it could seem to be worthless, except for the metallic value of the coins and recycled paper value of the currency.

However, the government guarantees that it will accept its coins and currency as payment for taxes. In other words, in addition to scarcity in supply relative to demand imbuing a value to our currency, requiring that taxes be paid in US dollars also creates additional value for our currency. Because taxes take a significant amount of most people's pay, this is a quite meaningful guarantee—one that gives money real value even without the backing of gold or other precious metals.

The real value of money is ultimately determined by its supply and demand. There will be times when the demand for money may slacken, and other times when the demand for money may surge. The Federal Reserve may allow a substantial increase in the supply of money during economic downturns, and, alternatively, attempt to cut back the money supply when inflation threatens. This is accomplished in open market operations by the New York Federal Reserve Bank in the buying and selling of federal funds that are borrowed overnight by banks to meet their requirements. This directly affects short-term interest rates, which are kept within a narrow range specified by the Federal Open Market Committee.[21]

Banks create money out of "thin air" when they initiate a loan to someone by creating a checking account funded by the money from another person's checking or savings account. The same money cannot be in two places at the same time, but it is. This makes it clear that banks are creating money every day, but they are limited in how much they can create by reserve requirements. In addition to setting reserve

---

21 In this author's opinion, the resulting yield curve is too flat in that long-term interest rates are unduly influenced by these short-term rates. For example, the ten-year interest rate is more closely correlated with the current federal funds rate than with the corresponding realized rate. In other words, the market's implicit time horizon for the ten-year rate is much shorter than ten years. Several other authors have expressed similar concerns.

requirements, the Federal Reserve is tasked with controlling the amount of money in circulation by buying short-term Treasury securities to increase the money supply or selling such securities to reduce the money supply. Alternatively, the Fed could create money out of "thin air" by creating checking or savings accounts for individuals, as long as it did so in moderation to avoid excessive inflationary pressure.

A system of establishing and maintaining ownership of money is essential to any successful currency. Originally, the physical possession of coins and paper notes was all that was necessary. Later, bank records were the basis for certifying ownership. More recently the blockchain technology has bypassed banks and established a collective memory for recording ownership. Transfer of ownership can take place over smartphones without bank or government involvement, as demonstrated in the M-Pesa system first widely used in Kenya and now spreading throughout the world, especially in developing countries.[22] The ultimate impact of these trending changes remains to be seen, but they must be taken into account as important factors affecting an economy.

WIN-WIN STRATEGY MAXIMIZES CIRCULAR MONEY FLOW

Think of a small, remote fishing village on an isolated island. The single family-owned restaurant, bar, and general store are at the center of economic activity. If the restaurant, bar, and store workers are not adequately paid, and the fishermen and farmers who supply the food are not adequately compensated, the general store, restaurant, and bar will not

---

22   In theory, the blockchain technology could be used to bypass government in establishing, maintaining, and changing other collective agreements such as marriage and adoption.

prosper. When the workers, farmers, and fishermen cannot afford to buy back the value they create, prices are too high or wages are too low.

When workers, farmers, and fishermen have lots of money to spend, they spend a lot at the general store, restaurant, and bar. The more they make, the more they spend. The workers, farmers, and fishermen have to keep up with demand. Getting more money means spending more and working more. When the money flow is good and the velocity of money is high, everyone is fully employed and producing at full capacity while consumers are flush with cash and eager to spend.[23] On the other hand, getting less money means spending less and working less. The store owner does better when the village as a whole does better.

Being tightfisted with the fisherman, farmers, and workers is the I-win-you-lose strategy. Saving a few bucks in the short run means losing a lot of money in the long run. The static fixed-pie strategy ultimately loses to the dynamic growing-pie strategy. Win-win wins and I-win-you-lose loses. "Us versus them" doesn't work. When the game is greed, we can all compete to see who can be the greediest, but when the game is generosity, we can all work together to produce more for everyone. To achieve this, we need either lower prices or increased wages.

On a remote island, a single family-owned general store, restaurant, and bar can easily see its self-interest in stimulating the island's economy by paying its workers and suppliers more until it achieves optimal money

---

23   This assumes a given amount of money in the system. Alternatively, in theory the amount of money in the system could be increased while holding the velocity of money constant. In reality, some combination of the amount of money and the velocity of money determines the level of demand and production. *If that combination is too low*, demand and production suffer and deflation triggers a downward spiral. Workers are reluctant to accept a wage cut, and consumers hold off on consumption in anticipation of even lower prices in the future. The economy gets stuck in a *liquidity trap* in rejecting negative nominal interest rates. *If that combination is too high*, inflation can become excessive.

flow, where all resources are fully utilized and the family business (and everyone else) is making maximum profit in real terms. However, in a larger economy, paying workers and suppliers more to maintain an optimal money flow becomes problematic. The overall economy is a common property resource facing a free rider problem, where every business would like to see other businesses pay their workers and suppliers more but not pay more itself.

In a larger economy, each business pursues its own self-interest in a manner similar to the overfishing problem in a commonly owned lake (or ocean in an international context). There are times when the optimal money flow can only be achieved by collective action (i.e., government stimulus). (The common property resource problem has been extensively analyzed by Elinor Ostrom[24] and Oliver Williamson,[25] for which they earned the Nobel Prize in economics in 2009.)

Another widely used example focuses on Henry Ford's strategy in 1914 of increasing the pay of the workers producing his Model T cars.[26] By Ford raising their pay to $5 for an eight-hour shift, the workers were able to gradually accumulate enough money to buy one of the $575 cars for themselves. Work at Ford's auto plant was long and hard; many workers quit before the wage increase. Yet that wage increase actually saved Ford money by reducing training and other turnover costs. This increased Ford's profits from $25 million in 1914 to $57 million two years later. In effect, Ford created his own little successful village of autoworkers.

---

24   Ostrom, Elinor. *Governing the Commons*. Cambridge: Cambridge University Press, 1990.

25   Williamson, Oliver. *The Mechanisms of Governance*. Oxford: Oxford University Press, 1996.

26   Reich, Robert B. *Aftershock: The Next Economy & America's Future*. New York: Vintage Books, 2011.

In theory, Walmart could learn from Ford's experiment in generosity and take the lead in raising wages when the economy is struggling. Walmart workers buy many of their household products from Walmart, and the plumbers, electricians, and bus drivers these workers employ in their daily lives probably spend a lot at Walmart as well. Traditionally Walmart workers have not been paid very well. There is no union at Walmart to demand higher pay. But Walmart should ask the following: If we pay our workers better, where will they spend a lot of the extra money? The most likely answer: at Walmart. Even much of the money those workers pay to a plumber to fix their toilet or to a roofer to fix their roof will probably end up back at Walmart sooner or later. When Walmart and similar major businesses take the lead in stimulating the economy, everyone can be made better off. In fact, in January 2018 Walmart did raise its starting wage to $11 an hour.

To be fair, we should note that Walmart is fighting off tech giant Amazon and is under pressure to keep its prices low. Even Walmart stores in remote rural areas face increasing price pressure from e-commerce.

MANAGING THE BUSINESS CYCLE AND MONEY FLOW

In the face of declining demand for its products and services, a business is unlikely to hire more workers and raise the pay of existing employees during an economic downturn to help stimulate the economy and bring it out of a recession. Microeconomic incentives direct businesses to do exactly the opposite. When faced with falling sales revenues, businesses are more likely to lay off workers, cut overtime pay, and freeze pay rates or even negotiate pay reductions. Although from a macroeconomic point of view businesses would be collectively better off with an increased money flow, each business pulls back in the face of reduced demand for its goods and services. In this situation the natural tendency of the system is to do exactly the opposite of what is needed. Again, microeconomic incentives drive the economy away from, rather than toward, a stable macroeconomic equilibrium. Instead of stabilizing itself in the rough seas, the ship rocks from side to side more and more until it flips over and sinks in a recession (or depression, in the absence of government intervention).

A business cycle is like a pendulum that goes too far in one direction, only to gain too much momentum in the reverse and overshoot equilibrium. Classical and neoclassical economists focus solely on the natural forces that ultimately bring the economy back toward equilibrium, but ignore, or at least discount, the natural forces that fed the momentum away from equilibrium in the first place. Unlike the traditional paradigms, the new money flow paradigm rejects the assumption that the economy will automatically adjust. Later we will discuss the role of government in providing automatic stabilizers to dampen these oscillations and bring the economy back to equilibrium more quickly.

CAPITAL'S TRIUMPH OVER LABOR

From a slow beginning in the 19th century, gradually accelerating advances in technology have favored fixed costs over variable costs. Our economy's transformation from labor intensive to capital intensive has been picking up speed. For a capitalist, the same amount of real investment dollars has produced greater productivity and a relatively high return on investment.

Almost any productive enterprise requires some amount of labor and some amount of capital. Increasing the proportion of labor relative to capital means more labor hours. But a single worker can only work so many hours. A larger proportion of labor means some combination of more workers and each worker working more hours. Increasing the money flow to labor most likely means increasing the demand for new products and services, because workers tend to have a high marginal propensity to consume.

Alternatively, increasing the proportion of capital increases the money flow to capital. But it does not necessarily increase the number of capitalists receiving that money flow. When more and more capital is owned by fewer and fewer people, and those people have a low marginal propensity to consume, that increased money flow to capital does not do much to increase the demand for new products and services. Without an increase in demand, no sensible business owner will invest in additional productive capacity. Business confidence comes with increased demand—not the other way around. Marketing consultants determine the potential demand for any proposed project. Many projects have failed because business owners did not accurately estimate demand in advance. "Build it and they will come" may work in *Field of Dreams*, but not in the real world. Read Lawrence Summers's book *The Post-Widget Society* for a deeper dive into the role of technology in our economy and the causes of this secular stagnation.[27]

Increasingly over time, more and more money flows to capital and less and less to labor. The capitalists get relatively richer and the laborers get relatively poorer and, in recent decades, absolutely poorer in real purchasing power. Thomas Piketty provides an exhaustive review of the evidence showing that over time the predominant flow of money has been upward, to the wealthiest elite class.[28]

Piketty's book raises two questions. The first question is, what is the underlying cause of this phenomenon? The second question is, what

27   Summers, Lawrence H. *The Post-Widget Society: Economic Possibilities for Our Children.* New York: Farrar, Straus & Giroux, 2021.

28   Piketty, Thomas. *Capital in the 21st Century.* Cambridge, MA: Harvard University Press, 2014.

should we do about it? Our preceding explanation about the unstoppable, insuppressible accelerating transition from a variable-cost (labor) economy to a fixed-cost (capital) economy, assisted by "pay-to-play" politics, helps answer the first question. But the second question requires a better understanding of how money flows in a healthy economy.

CIRCULAR MONEY FLOW KEEPS ECONOMY HEALTHY

George Cooper responded to Piketty in his book *Money, Blood and Revolution*,[29] which Cooper extended and recently republished under the title *Fixing Economics*.[30] Cooper recalled the theory of blood flow established by Galen (129–200 AD), who argued that blood flowed through the body in much the same way that sap flows up a tree and out to the tips of the tiny branches. Galen claimed that blood originated in the liver, with nutrients supplied by the stomach, and then flowed first to the heart, and then outward to the extremities, where it evaporated.

Galen's theory held sway for over a thousand years until 1628, when William Harvey (1578–1657) published *On the Motion of the Heart and Blood in Animals*,[31] where Harvey reported his experiments demonstrating that blood flowed around the body in a circular loop and did not evaporate at the body's extremities. Harvey saw that the veins were the collection system for blood, and the arteries were the distribution system in a circular loop.

Cooper argues that in a healthy economy, money is first pumped

29   Cooper, George. *Money, Blood and Revolution*. Hampshire: Harriman House Ltd., 2014.

30   Cooper, George. *Fixing Economics*. Hampshire: Harriman House Ltd., 2016.

31   Harvey, William. *On the Motion of the Heart and Blood in Animals*. Frankfurt, 1628.

upward by the natural winner-take-all tendency for the rich to get richer. This was true in caveman days when the big guy got as much of whatever he wanted, and under the kings, pharaohs, emperors, and tsars, as well as in our modern economy, as capital in the form of fixed costs comes to dominate over labor in the form of variable costs.

This natural tendency for money to accumulate at the top is similar to how the heart's right atrium receives blood from the rest of the body. But there is little incentive in the economy for the money to trickle down. Instead, for a healthy economy the government must act like the heart's ventricles working in concert and proper rhythm with the atrium to encourage an adequate distribution of wealth to all extremities and to also return to the heart.

A healthy economy requires both the upward flow of money to the economy's right atrium and an active government as the left ventricle to maintain adequate demand to grow the economy dynamically with increasing productivity. Basically, Cooper calls for using fiscal policy to reroute the money flow from the rich to the middle class and working class to restore balance in the economy and enhance productivity growth.

The key to stimulating demand in the economy is to understand what different people do with newly acquired money. The proportion of a person's new money that goes for consumption, as opposed to savings, is known to economists as that person's marginal propensity to consume. A recent paper by Christopher Carroll and colleagues estimated the marginal propensity to consume (mpc) of the wealthiest 20 percent of Americans to be about 8 percent, while that of the poorest 20 percent was estimated to be about 94 percent.[32] Other factors held

---

32   Carroll, Christopher, Jiri Slacalek, Kiici Tokuoka, and Matthew N. White. "The Distribution of Wealth and the Marginal Propensity to Consume." *Quantitative Economics*, Vol. 8 (2017): 977–1020.

constant, the government spending multiplier is 1 / (1 − mpc). Thus, for the wealthiest 20 percent, the government spending multiplier is 1.087. In contrast, for the poorest 20 percent, the government spending multiplier is 16.667.[33]

Ignoring the dramatic difference between the multipliers of the poor and the wealthy and aiming a government spending stimulus on the average person's multiplier reminds one of the old joke that "a statistician is someone who can put their left hand in freezing water and their right hand in boiling water and say, 'On average, I feel just fine.'" Clearly, if politicians are serious about getting the most bang for the buck, then they need to target their stimulus spending on the poorest 20 percent.

A properly functioning economy grows much more rapidly than one slowing, or even declining in real terms, as labor incomes fall, demand dries up, and the growth curve flattens and then declines. As the mechanism of economic modulation, Federal Reserve interventionist policies must apply the correct tool for the given environment. When the Federal Reserve is already keeping interest rates low by providing financial markets with high levels of liquidity, little is accomplished when wealthy families and large corporations pile up large, unused cash savings. Investments in plant, equipment, and employment (jobs) occur when consumer demand begins approaching the limits of existing productive capacity. A healthy economy requires an adequate money flow to those who will actually spend the money to maintain effective demand for goods and services.

The rich ultimately may gain greater wealth when wealth is dynamically redistributed than if they hold on tightly to their large piece of

---

33   Ramsey, Valerie A. "Can Government Purchases Stimulate the Economy?" *Journal of Economic Literature*, Vol. 49, No. 3 (2011): 673–685.

the pie. By allowing money to flow downward to people who will actually spend it, the rich sow the seeds of a more bountiful harvest. It is not surprising that the velocity of money and multiplier effects tend to be much higher for working-class and middle-class families than for wealthier families.

GOVERNMENT'S ROLE IN MAINTAINING GOOD MONEY FLOW

Expecting business to automatically respond by investing more as our economy declines into a recession is counterintuitive. Expecting a business to automatically pull itself out of a recession is naïve in ignoring the natural history of booms and busts and the natural tendency for wealth to accumulate at the top. Adding another production line when your business is unable to sell all it produces with its existing lines of production makes no sense. The direction of causality is clear. Business confidence grows as demand increases—and not the other way around. When money flows only upward to the elites, the economy stagnates. When there is also sufficient money flow downward to the workers, the economy thrives.

Government sets the rules at the heart of our economy. In a healthy body, blood flows upward to the heart, which then pumps it back out to our extremities and back again. The continual upward and downward flow of money makes for a healthy, efficient economy. Government is not peripheral to a free enterprise system. Under the new money flow paradigm, government is seen as the heart of any healthy free enterprise system. Government is essential to establishing the conditions for a healthy money flow to maintain course and speed and keep the ship from capsizing in the rough seas of a turbulent economy.

It is important to recognize the perverse nature of the free market's response to a downturn. At the micro level, when a business is faced with a significant drop in the demand for its products or services, it naturally cuts back work hours and jobs along with production. But this is exactly the opposite of what is needed to restore demand at the macroeconomic level. The economy needs more money flowing to workers to increase, not decrease, consumption at such times.

Those who assume that wages will quickly and automatically adjust fail to recognize, much less address, this problem. Their story—about cleansing the economic body of its sins through wage reductions in order to shrink the economy to match an inadequate money supply—fails to recognize the obvious solution of just increasing the money supply and making sure that more of that money flows to workers with high marginal propensities to consume.

Moreover, the businesses that are wiped out in economic downturns are not necessarily the weak or inefficient ones, just the ones with insufficient cash on hand to ride out the economic downturn. The reason that the businesses of Jeff Bezos and Elon Musk have survived is not because of their initial profitability but rather because of their enormous financial resources. The mom-and-pop stores that get wiped out in an economic downturn just don't have that type of money lying around to ride it out. Economic downturns allow large corporations with sufficient cash on hand to buy out their struggling rivals or drive them out of business by temporarily lowering prices. Instead of *creative* destruction, it should really be called *competition* destruction.

The destruction of small, efficient firms by large, inefficient ones is a natural phenomenon in our free enterprise system. This is a process I call *financialization*. For example, a small pizza restaurant in Michigan was selling pizzas that were extremely popular. The demand was so high that the firm started freezing pizzas to sell in local supermarkets. They built a frozen-pizza plant in Michigan that was so successful that they built another one in Alabama. But then a large company bought them out. The big company was under pressure from its shareholders to increase short-term profits. It was looking for ways to cut costs. It started using cheaper cheese and less marinara sauce. It skimped on the crust. Soon no one wanted the pizza, and they stopped making it. It was just one more casualty of the *financialization* process.

Of all the major existing economic paradigms, only the Austrian and Marxian paradigms recognize the inherent instability of the free enterprise system. However, the Austrians see government as just adding to the problem, while the Marxists see complete government control as the final solution. The other major paradigms, such as variations on the Keynesian and monetarist paradigms, typically see demand shocks or supply shocks as responsible for economic downturns, and government as an outside force that may need to be brought in to deal with these occasional unfortunate events.

The Marxian paradigm recognizes the free market's inherent dysfunctionality. But it throws the baby out with the bathwater by rejecting free enterprise entirely. Marx ignored the importance of incentives, moral hazard, and free riders. Marxism leaves little room for individual initiative or entrepreneurial activity.

The Austrian economists recognize the inherent and inevitable nature of economic booms and busts, but they consider these cycles as a cleansing process where Joseph Schumpeter's creative destruction eliminates the weak and inefficient businesses in a Darwinian survival-of-the-fittest struggle. They mistakenly assume that government has no major role to play in the efficient allocation of resources.

When a downturn is severe enough, just pumping more money into the financial markets through the New York Federal Reserve Bank's open market operations is not always effective. The current Federal Reserve system of monetary policy is too slow to avoid recessions when consumer demand is inadequate and too slow to avoid inflation when consumer demand is excessive. Manipulating the money supply by adjusting interest rates through open market operation in the New York financial markets is insufficient. As Ben Bernanke, Tim Geithner, and Henry Paulson conclude in their recent book, "Still, the current mix of constraints on the emergency policy arsenal is dangerous for the United States—and, considering the global importance of the US financial system and the dollar, dangerous for the world."[34] They point out that our politicians have not yet fully grasped the fundamental nature of the money flow problem.

A simple solution is to create Federal Reserve Bank accounts for every American age 18 or older with a Social Security number.[35] These accounts would facilitate direct cash payments, as proposed by Mark Blyth and Eric Lonergan in an excellent article in 2014 in *Foreign Affairs* magazine.[36] Such accounts could be referred to as "My America" prosperity accounts. In effect, these accounts could be used for direct cash transfers between individuals and/or businesses. If someone rakes your leaves or cuts your grass, you can pay them instantly (no check-clearing delay) using a direct cash-to-cash transfer from your "My America" account to their "My America" account.

Initially, the Fed would place $1,000 in each "My America" account,

---

34   Bernanke, Ben S., Timothy F. Geithner, and Henry M. Paulson Jr. *Firefighting: The Financial Crisis and Its Lessons.* New York: Penguin Random House, 2019.

35   Other papers that propose Central Bank Accounts include Berentsen, Aleksander, and Fabian Schär. "The Case for Central Bank Electronic Money and the Non-Case for Central Bank Cryptocurrencies." *Federal Reserve Bank of St. Louis Review*, Vol. 100, No. 2 (2018): 97–106. See also Ricks, Morgan, John Crawford, and Lev Menand. "A Public Option for Bank Accounts (Or Central Banking for All)." Vanderbilt Law Research Paper 18–33. UC Hastings Research Paper No. 287. June 6, 2018.

36   Blyth, Mark, and Eric Lonergan. "Print Less but Transfer More: Why Central Banks Should Give Money Directly to the People." *Foreign Affairs*, Vol. 93 (September/October 2014).

which cannot be withdrawn until after age 70. These accounts would be absolutely guaranteed with no counterparty risk. Allow individuals to add their own money to the account up to an annual limit and withdraw that money at any time along with any interest earned.

When consumer demand wanes and a recession looms, the Federal Reserve could inject more money directly into these "My America" accounts, money that individuals could withdraw at any time using their smartphones.

When inflation threatened, the interest rate on the accounts could be increased and the annual limit on individual contributions to the account could be raised to motivate consumers to delay consumption in favor of earning a good return on their money. After all, the whole purpose of interest rates is to get individuals to trade off current consumption for future consumption.

WEALTHY MAY GAIN FROM HEALTHY MONEY FLOW

In a vigorous economy, more money will flow through the hands of the elite than in an economy where the elite try to stop the money flow and hold on to every last dollar they can. Again, just as farmers invest in the spring to receive bountiful harvests in the fall, if corporations and wealthy individuals pay higher income and estate taxes, money can flow to middle-class and working-class Americans who will stimulate our economy through investments in education, health care, Social Security, infrastructure, and basic research. This might produce an even greater money flow back to business and the wealthy. The objective is not to diminish the wealth of the wealthy, but to make them even wealthier along with the rest of us. As every farmer knows, this requires investment.

Bill Gates and Warren Buffett understand the importance of contributing to the American dream for everyone, while ensuring that their own businesses thrive in a healthy and dynamically growing economy. They are proud to invest in the lives of others in the United States and throughout the world. They understand that the "us versus them" philosophy of greed only leads to a poorly performing economy producing well below its potential.

In a greedy world, the money flow dries up, and restaurants, stores, and other businesses go bankrupt. In a generous world, where an optimal level of taxation pumps money out to the poor and middle class, the elite benefit from the high demand for their goods and services. The I-win-you-lose, winner-take-all economy stagnates, while the win-win economy thrives.

The key is in determining the optimal money flow. The elite can make America great (again) by investing in America through their generous tax payments on the demand side and investments on the supply side to maintain a healthy level of supply and demand. Poor money flow results in the well-known *liquidity trap*,[37] where resources, especially labor resources, go unused, and equilibrium occurs only in a nonexistent, theoretical world of negative wages and negative interest rates.[38]

---

37   Krugman, Paul R. "It's Baaack: Japan's Slump and the Return of the Liquidity Trap." *Brookings Papers on Economic Activity*, No. 2 (1998): 137–205.

38   Real interest rates can be negative when nominal interest rates fall below the rate of inflation, but a negative nominal interest rate economy is not realistic for individuals. The Fed could apply a negative nominal interest rate on banks, but only because banks are *required* to hold reserve funds with the Fed.

INSUFFICIENT MONEY FLOW BLOCKS
YOUTH DEVELOPMENT

As explained previously, the broken link between sweat equity and the ownership of capital is systematically and inevitably causing more and more money to flow to the owners of capital and relatively less money to flow to workers. Families have tried to compensate for economic stagnation with both husbands and wives seeking full-time jobs. Elizabeth Warren explains how families with children drive up home prices in neighborhoods with good schools, often buying bigger and more luxurious homes than they can afford just to get a decent education for their children.[39] For many in the United States, working hours have been extended rather than shortened. People have taken on more and more debt to cover their expenses. Young people are putting off buying cars, getting married, having children, and purchasing homes. Some are living with their parents while paying off college debt. Movement out of rural areas into a revived urban core in major cities is cutting transportation costs and allowing apartment sharing to reduce expenses. Backyard and rooftop gardens have gained greater popularity and have helped reduce the cost of food. Ride sharing has become popular.

Money flowing to individuals providing various internet-related services, such as Airbnb, Uber, Lyft, and many, many more, does not provide that reliable paycheck or defined benefits. To compensate for inadequate compensation, young people have embraced sharing. It started with the sharing of music. Now newspapers, magazines, and books are being shared over the internet as e-books and audio books. More and more authors and artists are bypassing the middlemen and distributing their

---

39   Warren, Elizabeth, and Amelia Warren Tyagi. *Two-Income Trap: Why Middle-Class Parents Are Still Going Broke.* New York: Basic Books, 2003.

creations for free. People are offering to rent out rooms in their homes via such services as Airbnb while others offer rides in their cars and trucks via Uber or Lyft. Everything from tools to baby carriages is being shared through neighborhood social media sites, such as Nextdoor.

Despite these trends and efforts to compensate, insufficient money flow is hampering the professional development of young people. Young people are trapped in nine-to-five jobs to meet all their debt repayment obligations, instead of creating some new technology or launching a new internet startup business. This is not helping our economy grow.

Providing health care and basic needs could enable our young people to make use of their most creative and productive talents. Everyone wants to do great things. But coming up with the money to pay the rent and put food on the table may hold them back. Providing our youth with basic medical and financial security and a greater sense of empowerment and responsibility can enable them to grasp the multitude of opportunities that promise to extend and enrich their lives.

MONEY FLOWS THROUGH OUR NEW "GIG" ECONOMY

Traditionally a business provided its workers with a consistent and reliable paycheck along with defined health and retirement benefits. However, in recent years, even larger, well-established companies have switched to defined contributions instead of defined benefits. Obviously, this shifts the risk of economic and stock market volatility from companies to their employees, making their lives even more uncertain. It also undermines their motivation to ensure that they make their greatest and most effective effort in helping maximize their company's profits. When your company says that "you are on your own," it is saying that "we are not all in this together." This makes the break between sweat equity and the ownership of capital even worse in weakening employee motivation and morale.

Delinking company retirement benefits from the company's performance makes employees focus primarily on short-term contributions to the company's well-being and discourages long-term company planning. Greater employee mobility means less employee commitment. Family businesses used to treat employees as family in the context of a more permanent relationship, but today large corporations often treat employees as just another factor input.

Companies are employing more part-time and temporary employees than ever before. In place of traditional, full-time employment, our new "gig" economy has lessened our commitment to our labor force by reducing the total money flow to regular employees in favor of part-time and contingent workers who receive little, if any, employee benefits. A 2015 report from the US General Accountability Office[40] determined from the General Social Survey that over 40 percent of workers are contingent workers.[41] At our colleges and universities, the American Association of University Professors reports that 70 percent of the courses are taught by nontenured and nontenure-track employees.[42] These graduate students, adjunct professors, and full-time nontenured employees are often paid a small fraction of what their tenured counterparts are paid (e.g., $1,500 for a full-semester course at some smaller colleges).

---

40   Previously known as the US General Accounting Office.

41   See this May 25, 2015, article in *Forbes* magazine: https://www.forbes.com/sites/elainepofeldt/2015/05/25/shocker-40-of-workers-now-have-contingent-jobs-says-u-s-government/#382632df14be.

42   See the American Association of University Professors report: https://www.aaup.org/sites/default/files/Academic_Labor_Force_Trends_1975-2015.pdf.

"LIGHTS-OUT" MANUFACTURING: LESS LABOR, MORE CAPITAL

Labor and capital are increasingly no longer even operating under the same roof. The new trend is toward "lights-out" manufacturing where machines carry on in the dark without humans. Some systems manufacture the products and load them onto trucks in the dark without human intervention. Labor will be needed even less as driverless cars and trucks replace human drivers and algorithms replace knowledge workers.

In a similar shift away from human labor, 3-D printing is emerging as a direct source of physical production, able to customize products— and quickly deliver them directly to consumers via drones. Even a small business may soon see its delivery range extended by drones. Delivery of books, groceries, and other items by drone is already being developed. The pilotless air transport of people may be next. For example, it could replace the piloted helicopter transport of people between New York's Kennedy, LaGuardia, and Newark airports.[43]

Our economy is clearly morphing into one that not only separates capital from labor but also makes labor more of a distant cousin to capital instead of a close relative. It is no surprise that the return to labor is falling dramatically relative to the return to capital.

THE ROLE OF INFLATION IN PRODUCTIVITY GROWTH

There are two economic circumstances where employers tend to increase productivity. In the first circumstance, inflationary pressure in a full-employment economy provides employers with an opportunity to introduce

---

43   For example, go to https://www.volocopter.com/de/.

new technology without instigating layoffs. When demand is exceptionally strong and prices are rising along with revenues, an automobile company might introduce new technology in a factory while maintaining employment at current levels and holding wages down so that the increased revenues can be used to pay for the new technology. This is the traditional approach, and it's where most productivity increases have occurred in the past.

However, when both globalization and the rate and availability of technology improvements began increasing more rapidly over time, inflation did not develop to the point where real wages could fall adequately to pay for implementing the new technologies. Instead, employers had to wait for recessions. After laying off workers and waiting for the restoration of demand, employers used a new strategy of replacing the laid-off workers with new technology as their businesses emerged from recession.

This strategy was also effective in avoiding worker, union, or public objections and concerns. Since the new technology was not directly replacing particular workers (although former workers were not being called back), this strategy minimized bad publicity and did not undermine the morale of the current workforce.

In the first circumstance, the traditional approach to incorporating new technology involved allowing inflation to reduce the real wages of workers while maintaining or even increasing slightly their nominal wages. This approach worked at various times throughout the 1970s, 1980s, and 1990s. A moderate degree of inflation allowed us to have our cake and eat it too. Back then some new technologies could be introduced without laying off large numbers of workers, as long as inflation was rising sufficiently to significantly reduce the employers' wage bills and expand output in response to the excess demand. An employer wanting to add more workers in a full-employment economy will have to offer higher wages to get workers to quit their old jobs and sign on to new ones. If all workers are employed and I want to start a new Burger King franchise, I will need to offer a higher wage to convince workers at a nearby McDonald's or at other retail establishments to quit their jobs and join my business. Such a rise in wages means inflation of at least 2 percent. Some economists have argued that inflation should be around 4 percent to achieve a combination of moderate wage growth along with a robust adoption of new technologies.

However, there's always a concern that inflation might rise faster than improvements in technology and get out of hand. In the past, the Federal Reserve had to put the brakes on the economy by raising interest rates as a way to stop the possible development of runaway inflation. More often than not, this led to a significant downturn, including rising unemployment as the economy slipped briefly into recession. But globalization and the ever-faster implementation of increasingly cost-effective new technologies have prevented inflation from rising significantly. With sufficient economy-wide inflation, a business can raise its prices while holding down wages to enable it to accumulate enough additional revenue to afford a rapidly expanding array of new technologies without laying off workers. Without inflation, employers find it difficult to reduce the real wages of their employees. As John Maynard Keynes has pointed out, nominal wages are sticky downward. Holding nominal wages constant allows real wages to fall as prices rise. Consequently, employers must wait for either inflation or recession. Slow expansions without significant inflation prevent a more rapid introduction of new technologies and a consequent rapid improvement in productivity.

SUMMARY, OVERVIEW, AND TRANSITION

Thomas Piketty's *Capital in the 21st Century* presented the empirical evidence of how money flows primarily to capital and piles up at the top of the income and wealth scale. However, he did not reveal the underlying cause of this phenomenon. George Cooper developed the analogy between blood flow and money flow. In this chapter, I reviewed the nature of money and its role in the economy.

This chapter also emphasized the importance for both businesses and their employees of maintaining a healthy economy through good money flow. It discussed the common property resource aspect of good money flow. It also examined the free rider problem and the perverse nature of the free market's response to an economic downturn and the need for government to maintain a proper money flow. The new money flow paradigm points to the transition from variable costs (including labor) to fixed costs (including capital/machines) as the fundamental cause.

Most importantly, this chapter introduced the concept of creating "My America" Federal Reserve bank accounts, which are designed to replace the Fed's purchase of Treasury securities during an economic downturn. In sharp contrast to the various Keynesian and monetarist paradigms, the new money flow paradigm sees Fed policies that lower interest rates as contributing to or even promoting credit and debt bubbles that ultimately undermine the stability of our economic system by discouraging savings. The "My America" Fed accounts would avoid this problem by transferring money directly to average people to increase demand instead of spending much more money purchasing Treasury securities to lower interest rates in the hope that enough money will eventually trickle down. The next chapter will elaborate on how "coopetition" and a win-win strategy maximize the money flow and long-term growth rate of our economy.

CHAPTER 4

MONEY FLOW COOPETITION: "WIN-WIN" BEATS "I-WIN-YOU-LOSE"

Everyone wants to be a success in some way or another. Some people measure their success to some extent with money. But do they measure their success in relative or absolute terms? Relative success means keeping a boot on the heads of others to prevent them from rising above you. This assumes that the game is a zero-sum game, meaning one entity cannot be made better off without making another entity worse off.

Economists see this type of situation as a sort of tug-of-war, positioned along a contract curve in what they refer to as a Pareto optimal situation. Win-win is not possible in a zero-sum game or a Pareto-optimal situation. If you are winning, then I must be losing, and vice versa. Parties take turns in trying to undercut each other.[44]

Fighting in the Middle East demonstrates what happens when everyone plays I-win-you-lose. The use of airplanes and suicide bombers becomes an exercise in "I bomb your village and you bomb mine" repeated over and over. Nobody wins; everyone loses. The ultimate prize is one big pile of rubble. Some countries pick economic fights with others, not to win but to make sure that the other side loses.

In Charles Dickens's 1853 novel *Bleak House*, a family splits in two in a battle over the family fortune. Each side sues the other in an endless legal battle that goes on for years, and both sides end up worse off.

The same thing happens in our economy, but it's important to remember that the economy is not a fixed pie to be fought over. It's not a zero-sum game. A dynamic, growing economy can benefit everyone. It's a positive-sum game of win-win where everyone wins in absolute terms.

In the nuclear age, war makes the I-win-you-lose strategy ever more dangerous. Human survival may depend upon our willingness to find common ground and compromise. In our communities, as well as in our nation and in the world, we must work together for success.

WIN-WIN STRATEGY WORKS BEST FOR BUSINESS

I learned about the importance of the win-win approach when I returned home from military service in Vietnam. When I first went to Vietnam, the FBI checked out my past so that I could get a secret clearance to work

---

44   For an excellent discussion of how economic behavior differs for positional goods (e.g., luxuries) versus nonpositional goods (e.g., necessities), see Frank, Robert H. *The Darwin Economy: Liberty, Competition, and the Common Good.* Princeton, NJ: Princeton University Press, September 2011.

at US Army headquarters and Headquarters Company at Cam Ranh Bay Support Command in Vietnam.[45] Upon my return to the States, the secret clearance allowed me to get a position with Bendix Corporation's Aerospace Division as a subcontract administrator on some military projects and the Apollo moon mission.

At that time, I had a master's degree in economics but did not have much experience in business. We had contracted with an engineering company near Boston for some lenses. After the lenses arrived, I sent them out to the shop to have the engineers determine whether they met the required specifications. The engineers reported back that the lenses were unacceptable because they had vignetting (sharp at the center but fuzzy at the edges). I insisted that the company replace the lenses without any additional compensation. Following the I-win-you-lose mind-set, I figured that it was their mistake so they should pay to correct it. They were not happy about it when I insisted on sticking to the original contract price. They delivered replacement lenses that met the specifications.

Months later I realized my mistake in being so strict in following the I-win-you-lose strategy. When we needed additional lenses quickly and turned to the engineering company, they said that because they'd lost money on the previous contract, they didn't want to do any further business with us. I had to agree to renegotiate that earlier contract so they would not have a loss, then agree to a new contract that took into consideration the additional work needed to avoid the vignetting problem.

What I learned as a young man was that success in business requires

---

45 Most soldiers working at US Army headquarters were also members of Headquarters Company, but liaisons representing other units also worked at headquarters and were not members of Headquarters Company. See details at the "slideshare.net" website by searching for the terms "Marsh" and "Vietnam."

that your suppliers make a profit too. When your company does well, and your suppliers also do well, you have a good team. The I-win-you-lose strategy is for losers who don't know how to work well with others. In the business world, relationships are important, and that requires being somewhat flexible and generous in following a win-win strategy. Repeated bankruptcies can be a sign of a business leader who does not get along well with contractors and suppliers.

Often in business, maximizing profits in the long run requires not being too rigid and insistent on maximizing them in the short run. Long-term investments sometimes require short-term losses. Amazon ran losses for years before becoming a very large and very profitable business. Generosity in the short run—including paying your trading partners well—often pays off in the long run.

Thoughtful retailers have developed win-win strategies with their customers and their suppliers. Some stores offer their customers a slight discount for bringing their own containers, such as refillable bottles or bags. Starbucks reduces your bill by ten cents if you bring your own coffee mug. Whole Foods does the same when you bring your own bags. Uber, Lyft, and Zipcar provide you with transportation without the expense of purchasing and maintaining a vehicle. This is especially important for our young people in their high-debt and low-wage circumstances when their personal money flow seems more negative than positive.

Walmart is experimenting with a program to save customers' shipping charges, while augmenting their associates' pay, by having customers order items that are initially delivered to the nearest Walmart store but then delivered directly to the customer's house by employees on their way home from work. The normal direct-to-customer shipping charge is then split between the customer and the store employee. The win-win strategy helps people feel they are working well together with others on the same team. It is all part of the sharing economy. Restaurants tend to attract more customers in areas that have an assortment of eating establishments, and antique shops do better when there are other antique shops nearby. Your chamber of commerce helps all local businesses encourage and support one another in a win-win strategy.

WORKING TOGETHER SAVES RED BRIDGE SHOPPING CENTER

To appreciate the power of the win-win strategy, consider the case of the Red Bridge Shopping Center in Kansas City, Missouri. The long-time owner of the shopping center had lost interest in investing money in the upkeep of the shopping center. He had retired and moved to Florida. The shopping center was only 47 percent occupied, and the infrastructure was badly deteriorating. The movie theater had leaks in the roof that prevented the showing of any further movies, green slime was growing on the back section of the roof, electrical lines were worn and frayed, the cement curbs in the parking lot were crumbling, and the concrete was falling off the rebar in the loading dock. Property management companies had looked at the property and rejected it as any sort of reasonable investment.

But nearby residents remembered how great the shopping center had been in the old days and were eager to see it restored to its "glory days." The neighborhood association worked with their city council representatives and the local school system to try to find a new property management team. The Lane4 property management group finally showed some interest, in spite of the fact that they had earlier rejected the idea. Twice a busload of residents traveled to city development meetings to offer support.

Many residents indicated support for levying an additional sales tax through the Community Improvement District (CID) to help pay for improvements to the shopping center. The school district superintendent supported limits on the initial property taxes on any new property improvements made to the shopping center. Taxes on improvements would be eased in over several years under a tax increment financing (TIF) plan.

Residents also expressed a strong interest in frequenting new and existing businesses in the shopping center. Through this win-win strategy and with the help of their city council representatives, they were able to convince Lane4 to invest approximately $19 million into the purchase and renovation of the Red Bridge Shopping Center.

The key to the success of this win-win strategy in Kansas City was generosity. The residents showed their generosity by supporting the additional CID sales taxes and the TIF limits on near-term property tax increases on shopping center improvements. Lane4, for its part, showed its generosity in being willing to take on a tremendously risky investment in response to the widespread popular support for the project. The school system was willing to hold back on much-needed additional property tax revenues in order to allow the shopping center to be restored. Ultimately the success of the project was the work of the politicians, the nearby residents, the school system superintendent, and the Lane4 property group in a classic win-win strategy.

ECONOMIC DECISIONS NOT RATIONAL OR INDEPENDENT

The I-win-you-lose strategy can be expensive and irrational. Economists originally assumed that on average people were rational, independent decision makers. More recently, economists have come to realize that this assumption is systematically and profoundly wrong. Dan Ariely wrote the book *Predictably Irrational*, showing that not only were people irrational, but also their irrational behavior was systematic and predictable.[46]

In reality, people often deliberately take into account other people's interests and occasionally sacrifice their own self-interest to help others. Conversely, people may sacrifice their own well-being to prevent others from moving ahead of them in the economic order. This same behavior has been shown in animals such as monkeys who normally would accept a piece of cucumber as a reward for a task, but they rejected the cucumber when they saw other monkeys getting a grape for the same task. They would rather not get any reward than get a lesser reward for the same work.[47] Humans behaved similarly in what economists call the "ultimatum game."[48] We have an economic side to our behavior, but we also have a social side. Our sense of fairness can lead us to spend time, money, and effort differently than that predicted by traditional economic theory.

A relatively new field called "behavioral economics" has developed to help us better understand the economics of human behavior. Richard Thaler defied traditional economics with his book called *Misbehaving* promoting behavioral economics,[49] and in his earlier book with Cass Sunstein called *Nudge*.[50] It is surprising that economists took so long to understand and appreciate human irrationality when the people in marketing have understood and exploited it for hundreds of years.

The myth of the rational, independent decision maker has been

46   Ariely, Dan. *Predictably Irrational*. New York: HarperCollins, 2008.

47   See the YouTube video at https://www.youtube.com/watch?v=meiU6TxysCg.

48   Clark, Josh. "What's the Ultimatum Game?" How Stuff Works, https://money.howstuffworks.com/ultimatum-game.htm.

49   Thaler, Richard H. *Misbehaving: The Making of Behavioral Economics*. New York: W. W. Norton and Company, 2016.

50   Thaler, Richard H., and Cass R. Sunstein. *Nudge: Improving Decisions about Health, Wealth and Happiness*. New Haven, CT: Yale University Press, 2008.

debunked time and again. Contagion effects and irrational exuberance dominate. When I was a little boy, I thought that the prefrontal cortex (the thinking part of the brain) was the commanding general and that the limbic system (the emotional part of the brain) just followed orders. I was completely wrong. As with traditional economic thinking, I had it backward. Our emotions dominate, and our thinking brain is just an advisor, which often gets ignored in the rush to eat another jelly doughnut.

A lot of this irrational behavior is explained in Daniel Kahneman's book *Thinking Fast and Slow*.[51] Kahneman is the psychologist who won the Nobel Prize in economics in 2002. Kahneman's work reveals that the art-of-the-deal people are systematically shortsighted in focusing on changes in relative wealth rather than total wealth. For example, people were happier in a situation where their wealth increased from $1 million to $1.1 million than in a situation where they went from $4 million to $3 million. Obviously, a rational, independent decision maker would rather end up with $3 million than with only $1.1 million, but, as people become wealthier and their basic needs are satisfied, they are less motivated by absolute wealth and more motivated by relative wealth. Wealthy people compete to buy the most expensive properties, the most exclusive paintings, and the most expensive jewelry. They are not bothered by the rise and fall of the stock market, as long as other wealthy people are facing the same circumstances. Consequently, the incentives of wealthy people are not undermined by symmetrically applied income and wealth taxes, as long as their relative position in the *Forbes* list of the richest people is not altered.

Irrationality is frequently observed in situations where people spend a great deal of time and effort to get something for "free." They

---

51   Kahneman, Daniel. *Thinking Fast and Slow*. New York: Farrar, Straus & Giroux, 2011.

want to "win" at any cost. However, those who are intent on playing I-win-you-lose will sacrifice their own well-being and overall wealth to beat somebody at something, no matter what the cost. Revenge almost never pays off. It usually costs the person seeking revenge more than if they just let it go. For example, I could spend valuable time chasing after someone who let their dog crap on my lawn, or I could quickly remove the excrement and get back to writing this book. More often than not, when faced with a one-off insult or affront that is unlikely to be repeated, it is best to just let it go and move on. Behavioral economists and psychologists have performed many systematic experiments confirming these general conclusions.

Success in our economy is not about fighting over a fixed amount of money; success lies in maintaining an optimal money flow to ensure a healthy economy for everyone. However, money flow is not about a single simple, static policy; rather, it's about a set of dynamically changing policies that respond to the current state of the economy—as well as to the international economy and financial system. This in turn requires a political system that responds appropriately to the various states of our economy and a Congress that's not only aware of the effects of monetary and fiscal policies, but also willing to respond in a bipartisan manner to do what is best for the American people. Consequently, achieving an optimal money flow requires political, economic, structural, and operational changes in our government.

VELOCITY OF MONEY AND MULTIPLIER EFFECT

Is there a stronger multiplier effect for some sectors and some participants in the economy that can effectively increase the velocity of money as it flows through that part of the economy? Many authors point to Henry Ford, who doubled his autoworkers' pay to generate demand for his automobiles. Ford implicitly understood money flow. If there is no demand for your product, you lose. If almost everyone is buying your product, you win. And your workers win too. It becomes a win-win situation. You make them richer, and they make you richer.

Things look different during a recession, though. Typically, firms generate demand through advertising; but advertising alone may not be enough to generate sufficient demand during a recession. Even if intensive advertising during a recession increases the demand for your product somewhat, it may come at the expense of sales in other businesses.

To benefit the economy generally, the answer to keeping demand up during a recession is increased money flow. The key questions become as follows: When the economy is weak, how can the economy generate stronger money flow? Is there a particular multiplier effect for different sectors and different participants in the economy that can effectively increase the velocity of money as it flows through those parts of the economy? Are economic cycles inevitable, and, if so, what economic policies are appropriate at each stage of an economic cycle to counter these forces?

APPLYING MICRO SOLUTIONS
TO MACRO PROBLEMS

In the world of microeconomics, when you spend the money, it's gone! But when viewed from the lens of macroeconomics, when an individual spends money, the money is *not* gone. It just moves on. We often make the mistake of using microeconomic analogies to prescribe macroeconomic policies.

Saying "when you spend the money it's gone" may make sense for an individual or a business, or even for a particular governmental unit, but it is not a useful analogy for setting macroeconomic policy. In this context, when you pay for your food at the grocery store, the money goes to pay store clerks, to pay growers to replenish inventory, and to pay the rent, among other things. The real issue is how strong the overall demand is for goods and services relative to the productive capacity of the economy.[52] Weak and poorly distributed money flow can lead to an increase in unemployment, while an excessively strong money flow can trigger inflation. Understanding money flow is the key to avoiding recessions.

In keeping with the micro- vs. macroeconomic perspective, a balanced budget (micro) is not the same as a balanced economy (macro). Money flows through the economy in the way that blood flows through the body. Inflation is like an aneurism caused by too much money chasing too few goods. The pressure from the money flow builds up as it outstrips available goods and services. Alternatively, congestive heart failure—blockage—occurs when money piles up in corporate coffers. This can happen when investment opportunities are unavailable, because demand is inadequate. Why add more plant and equipment and employ more workers if you can't sell all of the product you are already producing?

A healthy economy requires the right balance between the flow of money going into demand and money going into investment. Too much demand leads to inflation. Too little demand reduces investment opportunities and leads to recession. When demand is too strong, the money flow needs to be directed away from consumption and into

---

52 Imports and exports must also be taken into account. Part of our productive capacity is used to produce exports. Imports help satisfy some of our demand for goods and services without requiring additional productive capacity. There are times when some markets being out of equilibrium (e.g., imports greater than exports) can compensate for other markets being out of equilibrium (e.g., more demand for goods and services than productive capacity to supply those goods and services). The *theory of the second best* tells us that trying to force equilibrium in one market (e.g., balance imports with exports) can make matters worse rather than better. For example, if imports are helping to satisfy demand when our economy is already at productive capacity, restricting imports to balance exports can lead to inflation.

investment. When demand is too weak, more money needs to flow to consumers to spend.

As mentioned earlier, poor people have a much higher marginal propensity to consume than rich people. When a poor person gets additional money, they are more likely to spend it. A rich person already has lawn service, nice clothes, and as many top-of-the-line automobiles and trucks as they may want. Giving a rich person more money typically results in more savings and investments, while a poor person is more likely to purchase more goods and services.

Achieving optimal money flow requires selecting from a number of possible ways of distributing the money. Infrastructure spending will have a much different effect than tax cuts, especially if the tax cuts primarily benefit special interests, including wealthier individuals who will likely not be putting that savings into more goods and services. An important aspect is generally knowing where the money is going and whether it will be used primarily for consumption or investment.

In addition, the multiplier effect and velocity of money reveal the full impact of an increase in money and how quickly the money will pass from one person or entity to the next person or entity. The velocity of money is different along each path with a different multiplier effect, so tracing the flow of money is important to determine the ultimate impact of any given economic policy.

TREATING GOVERNMENT AS OUTSIDE THE SYSTEM

Even though government is a major component in the functioning of an economy, some analysts treat government as an outside force that is exogenous to the operation of the economy. Pretending that government is exogenous, or should be exogenous, is not a realistic way to analyze and understand the economy. As an arm of the government, the Federal Reserve does not make decisions independently of the behavior of the economy. Although the Fed, as currently structured, has a limited and somewhat restricted tool kit to influence the economy, it is not too hard to anticipate how it will react to particular economic conditions. Ceteris paribus—other conditions remaining the same—the Fed will *raise* short-term interest rates when excessive inflation threatens. On the other hand, when recession looms, the Fed will make more money available in the Treasury securities markets and rates will *fall*. Any mathematical model of the economy must take the government's behavior into account in forecasting economic outcomes. Anticipating government policy action is part of the economic theory of *rational expectations*.[53]

The biggest flaw in economic thinking is in assuming that adding up choices at the individual or microeconomic level will inform us about the correct policy to pursue at the macro or economy-wide level. A simple example, provided earlier, called the *paradox of thrift*, explains that when everyone tries to save more during a recession, the total amount of savings falls instead of increasing. Libertarian Robert Nozick argued that the late basketball star Wilt Chamberlain becoming wealthy when each of his fans paid him reflects each individual's free will and, therefore, must be optimal overall. This argument is refuted by the arguments of Thomas C. Schelling in his book *Micromotives and Macrobehavior*. Schelling uses the example of hockey players who

53   Lucas, Robert. "Expectations and the Neutrality of Money." *Journal of Economic Theory*, Vol. 4, No. 2 (1972).

individually would not wear helmets, but collectively vote to require that helmets be worn by all players.[54]

The biggest flaw in economic thinking is treating government as an exogenous actor. Our collective set of preferences cannot be determined by simply adding up our individual preferences, which economists call our utility function. Kenneth Arrow showed in his *impossibility theorem* that this is due to not being able to add my units of utility to your units of utility in a meaningful way, but also to the whole being greater than the sum of the parts. Too often government is treated as an alien force from outside the perfectly competitive world of economics, a force that interferes with the efficient allocation of resources.

But a utility function is just a concept that economists made up to express our willingness to pay for things regardless of whether they are useful or not (e.g., a pet rock) or in our best interest or not (e.g., a dangerous illegal drug). From an economist's point of view, it is a positive as opposed to a normative concept. It is not a goal to be imposed on the individual but a concept to capture and summarize the individual's actual behavior.

Revealed preference is based on this conception of a utility function. By the same token, we can conceive of a national utility function that expresses our willingness to pay for another aircraft carrier. Arrow was correct that this utility function cannot be derived directly from our individual utility functions. But that doesn't explain the choice of an aircraft carrier. Such a choice can be captured in a national utility function.

As a nation, we have a utility function that reflects our choices as a whole. We should recognize our national utility function just as we

---

54   Schelling, Thomas C. *Micromotives and Macrobehavior*. New York: W. W. Norton & Company, Inc., 1978 and 2006.

recognize the utility function of another person in a financial transaction. Unlike social welfare functions that express welfare goals, the national utility function merely reflects the trade-off decisions involved in deciding how much of the nation's resources go into military spending as opposed to education or infrastructure spending, et cetera. In this sense, the national utility function is similar to an individual's utility function where no judgment is made about the usefulness or virtue of a pet rock or an illegal drug.

Our national desire for another aircraft carrier is not explained in our voluntary individual allocation of money, but is, in theory, expressed in our votes and those of our democratically elected representatives. When it is time to pay taxes, we do not decide how much we would like to pay the government this year. That choice was made together with our fellow citizens through the democratic process. But a national utility function makes sense just as surely as each of us has an individual utility function.

There exists a contract curve that defines the Pareto optimal points representing the trade-off between maximizing our own individual utility and maximizing the utility of the nation as a whole. The Pareto optimal trade-off plays out when we want to pay less in taxes but get more in government services. That might work in eliminating inefficiencies when we are off of the contract curve, but not when we reach it.

At every level of government, taxation and expenditures reflect the voters' joint utility function. In some cities you have a choice between paying the city to pick up your trash or having a private contractor pick up your trash. I have a neighbor who offers to take my leaves and yard waste to the city dump for a small fee. Why would we treat the neighbor and the contractor as legitimate economic actors who do not disrupt the efficient allocation of resources, but insist that the government is an external force that creates deadweight loss in almost every situation? We shouldn't. Rather, if the government actions reflect the joint utility function of the voters, then the voters are acting through their government just like my neighbor who gets some pleasure from helping me and some benefit from the small amount he charges me for the trash removal.

By choosing to live in a particular municipality, I am implicitly or explicitly entering into a contract to be bound by the decisions based on the joint utility function of that municipality's voters. Positive and negative externalities are then internalized such that correcting for them becomes part of the formalized social contract with my fellow citizens. Government then is no longer an external, alien force but a legitimate, albeit powerful, economic player in the story of efficient resource allocation in our economy.

If a governmental unit is the only entity providing a product or service (e.g., national defense), then it should be treated in economics as a monopolist. But instead of maximizing profits, it is maximizing the voters' utility function. If it is the only buyer (e.g., fissional material exclusively used for nuclear bombs), then government should be viewed as a utility-maximizing monopsonist—a single buyer of labor in a specific market, as in a monopsony. The industrial organization of the public sector can be just as complicated as that of the private sector.

Recognizing national, state, and local governmental utility functions certainly complicates economic analysis, but it incorporates government into the world of economics in a more meaningful way. This requires rewriting economics textbooks to treat government as a legitimate player with its own utility function and not an outside force disrupting the efficient equilibrium established by the legitimate players.[55]

---

55 Hopefully, eventually we will have to add an international utility function, if the United Nations and/or other international organizations reach a point where they achieve a meaningful ability to both command resources and make expenditures in a manner that in some sense reflects the will of the people through their national representatives. Combatting climate change and governing the world's oceans along with avoiding incoming asteroids and extending human civilizations throughout the universe may ultimately bring this into reality.

CONTAGION EFFECTS AND
IRRATIONAL EXUBERANCE

Some markets are dominated by variation in supply, such as many of the commodity markets. The classic "hog cycle" taught in standard introductory economics courses explains how this works. When hog prices get too high, farmers invest in more hog production, which ultimately leads to an oversupply of hogs. The prices of bacon and pork fall in response to the oversupply. Farmers then cut back on hog production due to the low prices, and the hog cycle begins again. Recently a similar cycle took place in the egg market, where an oversupply of eggs drove down the price of eggs. The saying that "the solution to high prices is high prices, and the solution to low prices is low prices" works well in solving the immediate problem of prices that are too high or too low, but it does not address the instability of such volatile markets.[56]

Government policies that interfere with these price adjustments are often ineffective and counterproductive. In the case of supply instability, the long-term solution is to look for ways to help the markets be more responsive to small price changes and to more accurately predict future price changes to avoid extreme variations in price. Future markets and crop price insurance contracts are helpful in this regard, but we need to make better use of artificial intelligence algorithms to better anticipate changes in global weather patterns and other, otherwise exogenous, factors to predict future price changes.

While the supply side of markets is usually dominated by key players with enough experience to anticipate, to some degree, the future price variations, the demand side often consists of a multitude of consumers who may be less able to anticipate future price changes, especially

---

56   Abbott, Chuck. "Trump Proposes 33% Cut in Crop Insurance." *Successful Farming* at Agriculture.com. February 13, 2018. https://www.agriculture.com/news/business/trump-proposes-33-cut-in-crop-insurance.

in markets where individual purchases are less frequent and constitute a smaller portion of the household budget expenditures. In these cases, the "high prices solve high prices and low prices solve low prices" solution does not work as well.

On the other hand, the stock market is an example where the demand for stocks often responds more rapidly than does the supply of stocks, leading to contagion effects driven by variations in demand rather than due to any significant changes in supply. Rather than cutting back stock purchases in response to higher prices, investors may increase their investment expenditures more rapidly as prices rise, in anticipation of even greater increases in valuations. Retail investors are most likely to get caught up in such momentum stock trading, while the companies themselves typically do not issue new shares of stock just to counter such increases in demand.

A "Giffen good" is one in which the usual law relationship of demand to price is inverted; rather than lower prices leading to greater demand, demand for a Giffen good actually decreases as its price goes down. Often this is the result of the so-called income effect, which overwhelms the effect of lower prices. Introductory economic explanations frequently use the Irish potato famine in the 19th century as an example where the fall in the price of potatoes reduced, instead of increased, demand for potatoes. This occurred because the lower price gave consumers enough money to reduce their dependence on potatoes and broaden their diets to include other foods.

In a more dynamic example of a similar effect, higher stock prices can induce investors to buy more instead of less stock, because of the income effect of higher stock prices on their overall wealth. Or, to put it another way, the excitement of seeing your stock portfolio rise in value may cause you to sell jewelry, real estate, and other assets, as well as using margin to buy more stock.

This suggests a different type of good that responds dynamically to expected price increases rather than statically to the current price. This type of good is similar to, but somewhat different from, a Veblen good, where the exclusive nature of a luxury good causes its price to rise and makes it more desirable. The Veblen good, like the Giffen good, is based on static price and quantity comparisons as opposed to the dynamic effect of responding to price increases in anticipation of even higher future prices.

Two extreme alternatives are available for thinking about our free market system. At one extreme, there are those who only see goodness and virtue coming from free enterprise where people behave rationally in pursuit of their own self-interest, which ultimately leads to everyone being made better off. Alternatively, there is the other extreme interpretation that sees greedy self-interest exploiting irrationality and contagion effects to constantly undermine the stability and benevolence of the system whenever it tries to establish some sort of stable equilibrium. In some circumstances, arbitrage leads to a quicker return to equilibrium, whereas in other circumstances, market manipulators can exacerbate disequilibrium. Technical analysis, instead of political ideology, is needed to differentiate between these two phenomena.

SUMMARY, OVERVIEW, AND TRANSITION

This chapter explored the interrelationships inherent in our economy, formally as expressed in government and informally in business-to-business transactions, and how market participants interact with other market participants in coopetition to determine the money flow that results in efficient market outcomes.

continued

The money flow paradigm treats government as the heart of the economy, with a legitimate utility function and a key role in maintaining money flow in an otherwise naturally unstable free market economy. The misguided tightfisted "greed is good" interpretation of Adam Smith leads to poor money flow and business failures, while the more generous "win-win" approach promotes successfully profitable businesses through cooperation and teamwork.

The new money flow paradigm rejects the idea that usually the free market by itself will maintain good money flow and efficient resource allocation, and government intervention is only needed under unusual circumstances, such as exogenous demand or supply shocks.

In the next chapter, we will examine the role of government in overcoming the common property nature of our economy by working with market participants to adjust money flow to match marginal costs to marginal benefits to bring about efficient resource allocation, greater economic productivity, and maximum economic growth for a healthy economy.

CHAPTER 5

GOVERNMENT: MATCHING MARGINAL COSTS AND BENEFITS

U nder our free enterprise system, government and private enterprise must play their proper roles to achieve efficient resource allocation. Positive externalities, negative externalities, public goods, and common property resources, as well as monopolies, oligopolies, monopsonies, and oligopsonies, require public or private collective adjustments to properly match marginal benefits to marginal costs. The problem is not too much government or too little government, but rather getting the optimal amount of government in just the right places for just the right amount of time. Simplistic policies that either throw money at a problem or, conversely, starve the beast (i.e., the government) are unlikely to provide optimal solutions.

ASYMMETRIC INFORMATION DISTORTS MARKET OUTCOMES

George Akerlof won the Nobel Prize in economics in 2001 for developing different aspects of the theory of asymmetric information in markets, which can lead to market failure. Traditional economic theory assumes transparency and complete information in all market transactions. Government can often play a constructive role in helping correct for such distortions. An obvious example is not allowing the use of insider trading information in the stock market. Another is requirements for disclosing certain facts, such as expenses and fees in financial markets or providing accurate mileage figures in the used-car market.[57]

Often buyers are at a disadvantage in not having as much information about a product or service as the seller. Buyers of labor services, such as trucking companies, benefit from the government issuing of commercial driver's licenses, which certify or signal the individual's qualifications that would otherwise be known with certainty only by that individual. Governments directly provide or sponsor such licensing in occupations with unusually hazardous working conditions and in many occupations requiring interaction with the public.

Conversely, there are times when the buyer has the upper hand, such as in purchasing health insurance, where the individual buying the insurance is likely to know more about their own health than the insurance company selling the insurance contract. This uncertainty leads to unduly high prices for health insurance. The Affordable Care Act was designed to address this problem by requiring that all citizens, both healthy and sick, sign up so that insurers could be assured that the participants in

---

57   Akerlof, George A. "The Market for 'Lemons': Quality Uncertainty and the Market Mechanism." *Quarterly Journal of Economics*, Vol. 84, No. 3 (1970): 488–500. doi:10.2307/1879431.

their insurance pools accurately reflected the average health of the population—rather than being subject to adverse selection, which is a special case of the biased sample selection problem.[58]

What this all adds up to is the realization that government is not some external force interfering with some autonomous and independent free enterprise system. Instead, government provides the foundation for the free enterprise system.

AN IMAGINARY WORLD THAT DISTORTS AND DENIES REALITY

There are two worlds. There is the imaginary world and the real world. In the imaginary world, government plays a very minor role and individuals pursue their own self-interests for the benefit of everyone. I love this world. It is a simple world. It places free enterprise at the heart of our economic, social, and political system, and rewards hard work and creative entrepreneurial investments. Competition drives businesses and their employees to work together to produce products of increasing quality at ever-lower prices. It is a very democratic world. Everyone is necessarily a consumer who can purchase most anything without regard to race, creed, color, gender, sexual orientation, transgender status, national

---

58 Nobel Prize laureate James J. Heckman was the first to develop an effective way of correcting for biased sample selection. Heckman, James. "Sample Selection Bias as a Specification Error." *Econometrica*, Vol. 47, No. 1 (1979): 153–161. doi:10.2307/1912352. JSTOR 1912352. MR 0518832.

origin, or ethnicity.[59] Workers and businesses trip all over one another trying to satisfy the consumer, who does nothing except benefit from the turmoil. Everything operates properly and automatically in this world. The economy automatically adjusts quickly to supply shocks and demand shocks. Government's role in this world is more or less limited to national defense and the enforcement of contracts. Everything else is privatized to avoid bureaucracy and inefficiency.

Economists have carefully examined this imaginary world and have unfortunately found a large and substantial number of flaws in it. First of all, efficient resource allocation assumes adequate competition and the availability of accurate price and product information. It also assumes that on average businesses, workers, and consumers are rational, independent decision makers who will adjust their behavior, at least on average, to changing market forces and conditions.[60] It does not adequately allow for contagion effects and systematic mistakes that affect entire markets, and, ultimately, the country and world as a whole for extended periods. It assumes that businesses, workers, and consumers have full information and an unlimited amount of mental energy, at least on average, to calculate and recalculate every economic decision they face. No

---

59   There are some people who argue that it is their religious right or obligation to discriminate against others on the basis of some private, personal characteristic. However, a business transaction is subject to contract law and other regulations. It is an economic transaction that is qualitatively different from a social transaction, such as giving someone a gift. Discrimination in economic transactions is not allowed under the law. Social transactions are very different from economic transactions. Don't try to pay your mother-in-law $50 for the great Thanksgiving dinner she made for your family. It will not be appreciated. People with poor social skills often do not understand the difference between an economic transaction and a social transaction.

60   See Dan Ariely's book *Predictably Irrational* (New York: HarperCollins, 2008), where he reports on careful scientific experiments that show that not only do people behave irrationally, but their irrationality is sufficiently systematic and consistent that it can be accurately and reliably predicted.

large, substantial group is ever tricked, deceived, or conned to any significant degree for any significant amount of time in this imaginary world.
In any case, markets always quickly and automatically adjust to any flaw
found in this imaginary money flow system.

This is not just about one-off cases as in the Bernie Madoff affair,
but system-wide distortions—such as the distortions that arose from
using various financial derivatives in real estate markets, which led to the
2007–2008 financial crisis.[61] Ever since the invention of money, there
have always been distortions and disruptions that have produced panics
and recessions, not to mention an extended and extreme countrywide
and worldwide depression.

Common sense suggests that we should try to anticipate possible distortions and take effective action to prevent them rather than assuming
that they won't happen here or won't happen again. Just as a prudent
family plans for possible job loss, health emergency, accident, or losses
from fire, tornadoes, or hurricanes, so to as a nation we should plan for
disruptions to our economy so we can respond more quickly and effectively to maintain proper money flow for a healthier, more stable economy over the long run.

As discussed earlier, one long-term cause of income inequality is the
natural tendency for wealth to accumulate at the top as a result of the transition from a largely labor-intensive economy to a largely capital-intensive
economy. This tendency directs more and more wealth to the owners of
capital and relatively less wealth to workers.

---

61   The poorly devised failed mortgages occurred in the private sector. Attempts to blame
     Fannie Mae and Freddie Mac, which merely repackaged existing mortgages as mort-
     gage-backed securities, are unconvincing. The financial crisis of 2007–2008 was largely
     due to and ultimately triggered by the creation and sale of aggressively marketed mort-
     gages. The mortgages that defaulted were created in the private sector.

Yet another important cause of income inequality is the decline of the old aristocracy and the rejection of *noblesse oblige* by the *nouveau riche*[62] and its replacement with the "pay-to-play" system as previously mentioned. The old "Eastern elite," who were primarily descendants of the Founding Fathers, maintained a low profile while exhibiting a strong sense of duty to serve others, or at least to not blatantly tout their wealth and exploit others. Their collective memory of the French and Russian Revolutions kept them from getting carried away in amassing or displaying too much wealth.

However, in the early 20th century, new capitalists emerged, such as John D. Rockefeller and Andrew Carnegie, who ignored *noblesse oblige* and accumulated vast wealth. They eventually learned from popular outrage and government antitrust action that they needed to reroute the money flow back to the people through their family foundations. More recently, Bill Gates and Warren Buffett have learned from history and instead followed *noblesse oblige* by focusing on helping others through the Gates Foundation.

POSITIVE AND NEGATIVE EXTERNALITIES

A fundamental requirement for the efficient allocation of resources is that marginal benefits match marginal costs. How does this work when your child is at risk of acquiring a dangerous, but noncontagious, disease? You may decide to pay to vaccinate your child against this disease. You decide how much of your limited resources, mainly time and money, should be allocated to vaccinating your child against a particular disease based on the potential benefits you, your child, and your family will receive from

---

62   Deneen, Patrick J. *Why Liberalism Failed.* New Haven, CT: Yale University Press, 2018.

such an investment in your child's health. The marginal expected costs will match the marginal expected benefits.

But what if the disease is highly contagious and your child is attending school or is otherwise out in the community at various activities? Your marginal cost allocation may not be sufficient, because you are only taking you, your child, and your family into consideration. The entire community has an interest in your child's, and every child's, vaccination when the vaccination is for a disease that is highly contagious. This is clearly a case of a positive externality. You still get to make the final decision on whether or not to vaccinate your child. However, the full marginal benefits, including the marginal benefits to other children, of your child's vaccination must be taken into consideration to match marginal benefits and marginal costs in this situation. This implies a fair and systematic collection of money (i.e., taxation) from community members to help pay for your child's vaccination. Or, to put it another way, the government should offer the vaccinations at a reduced, subsidized price.

In an example such as this—and many others—money must flow to the government in the form of taxes to allow the government to correct for this positive externality. In other words, a contagious disease creates a positive externality. Government must intervene to correct this defect in the free enterprise system to ensure an efficient allocation of resources. Simply put, in this circumstance, equilibrium cannot be achieved—where marginal benefits match marginal costs—without government intervention.

Here's another case in point. Until recently, Kansas City, Missouri, and many other cities required that homeowners pay to repair the sidewalk in front of their home. Homeowners were billed if they did not properly maintain that stretch of sidewalk and the city had to pay a contractor to fix the sidewalk. This is again a clear case of a positive externality. Young joggers, elderly walkers, and parents pushing baby carriages all benefit from that well-maintained stretch of sidewalk. The marginal benefits will not match the marginal costs if the benefit to the homeowner is the only one taken into account. Again, we find another case of positive externalities—where proper money flow means more government "interference," with taxpayers helping to pay for the maintenance of that stretch of sidewalk. Like the vaccinations, this is another situation where optimal government taxation and expenditure leads to a more efficient allocation of resources. There are many such cases of positive externalities requiring government intervention to ensure that marginal costs match marginal benefits, yet where the free enterprise system—with no government intervention—would otherwise lead to inefficient resource allocation.

But there are also many cases of negative externalities. Unlike positive externalities, instead of excess benefits accruing to the community as a whole, negative externalities impose excess costs on the community due to activities that *fail* to take those extra, unassigned costs into account. This is important because it means that marginal benefits are not matching marginal costs, and, therefore, resources are not being allocated efficiently. Again, the free enterprise system is unable to bring about efficient resource allocation without community (i.e., government) involvement. Water and air pollution are the most obvious examples of negative externalities, but such externalities exist wherever there are unaccounted costs beyond those being taken into account by the entity generating those costs. To an economist, the objective is not to eliminate pollution but, rather, to correct the free market's inefficient allocation of resources. In other words, the goal is not zero pollution, but, instead, the goal is to achieve an optimal level of pollution. It is the government's responsibility to properly assign the extra costs by imposing taxes on the units of output directly associated with generating those costs, and, thus, bring marginal benefits and marginal costs back into alignment.[63]

COMMON PROPERTY RESOURCES

An even more interesting money flow problem where the free enterprise system runs into difficulties is the common property resource problem. For example, wild fish swimming freely in the ocean serve as a common property resource for all of humanity. No nation or set of nations controls the oceans. Even if every square inch of ocean were privatized, it would be impractical and harmful to prevent fish from moving freely throughout the oceans. Consequently, a natural conflict exists between the interests of individuals competing to catch fish of various types and the overall interest in maintaining fish populations and avoiding over-fishing and extinction.

If the oceans were under a single private enterprise, then the long-term marginal costs could be matched with the long-term marginal benefits. But each individual or group acts in accordance with their own self-interest and catches fish without reservation, because if he or she does not, some other individual or group will take those fish anyway. There is no point in restricting one's own behavior if others do not do the same.

Again, a private solution is not practical for this problem, so some sort of public solution is needed; in this case, such a solution is needed if we want to maintain an economically viable ecology in the oceans of our world. Because the free enterprise system so clearly fails in this endeavor,

---

63   Note that absolute zero air pollution would require that we all quit breathing, because breathing emits carbon dioxide into the atmosphere. The real issue is not zero pollution but maintaining a sustainable, human-friendly environment.

in order to allow for efficient resource allocation, we need an international agreement—with the ability to *enforce* such an agreement.

An interesting exception to the need for government to maintain an optimal level of marine life is the lobster population. Because lobsters live near the coastlines, it's possible to create a quasi-form of privatization. In some coastal areas, "lobster gangs" are formed by local lobstermen who enforce their rules by cutting lines and/or removing unlicensed or unapproved traps, or even the lobsters in those traps. This informal and unofficial activity can, in fact, correct the excesses of the free enterprise system and solve the overfishing of lobsters. The problem with this extrajudicial system is that it's outside the bounds of the law and can result in violent confrontations. Just because "lobster gangs" can sometimes work efficiently in maintaining an optimal lobster population doesn't mean these gangs will always operate in our best interest. Instead, state and local laws and regulations provide better alternatives.

Of course, privatization could work for a lake that was owned by a single entity able to restrict its use under the law. In that case, the free market could potentially provide an optimal allocation of resources without the need for government intervention (beyond the usual laws protecting private property). However, the common property resource problem presents a thornier issue when privatizing is not practical. Competitive businesses offering privately operated, restricted-access alternative streets with their own water and sewer lines, for example, would not be practical, nor would they be an efficient use of resources. In this case, it makes more sense for government to provide these services, and for taxpayers to foot the bills.

DEALING WITH THE FREE RIDER PROBLEM

Boundaries between cities, states, and nations present the most frequently discussed "free rider problem"—in which nonpaying users benefit from a resource that's provided and paid for by others. Overcoming this problem can be tricky. It is often too costly to prevent an outsider or visitor from using (benefiting from) services or improvements paid for by the local citizens. Streets and police protection are two obvious examples that visitors use at little or no expense. Sometimes this is mitigated by income taxes paid by out-of-state or out-of-city workers or sales taxes paid by tourists. Efforts in some state legislatures (e.g., Missouri) to free out-of-city workers from paying a city (e.g., Kansas City) earnings tax under a no-taxation-without-representation rationale exacerbate this free rider problem and promote greater economic inefficiency with a larger cost-benefit mismatch.

THE ECONOMIC EFFECTS OF MINIMUM WAGE LAWS

One area of controversy that has been discussed widely is the establishment of minimum wage laws—passed by cities, states, and entire countries.

In theory, setting a higher wage should cause business to both reduce its demand for labor and raise the prices on its products to help cover the additional expense. Surprisingly, however, empirical evidence has not consistently supported this expectation. In one case, Seattle raised its minimum wage from $9.47 an hour to as much as $11 in 2015 and $13 in 2016. This increased average hourly wages by 3 percent, while reducing the number of related jobs by 9 percent.[64] However, a recent broader-based study of 137 minimum wage increases between 1979 and 2016 showed that the number of jobs lost closely matched the additional number of jobs gained.[65]

These studies did not take into consideration the timing of the business cycle of these minimum wage increases. Such an increase, when the economy is booming and unemployment is low, may be quite different from the response at the opposite end of the business cycle. Also, relatively small minimum wage increases may primarily impact the fast-food industry, which often pays new workers at or near the minimum, while manufacturing may pay unskilled workers a bit above the prevailing minimum and may only be affected by somewhat larger increases.

Two other factors may help explain the muted response to minimum wage increases: (1) labor is not uniform (some workers are more productive than others), and (2) workers work harder when faced with a combination of higher pay and more competition for their jobs. The first point reflects the fact that very low wages attract the least productive workers. Such workers may have problems getting along with others, including both the customers and their fellow workers. They may show up late for work or miss work entirely on some days. Other workers may have great potential but are not well motivated at such a low wage. This phenomenon is known to economists as *efficiency wages*. When people feel that they and their work are valued, they are

---

64   Jardin, Ekaterina, Mark C. Long, Robert Plotnick, Emma van Inwegen, Jacob Vigor, and Hilary Wething. "Minimum Wage Increases, Wages, and Low-Wage Employment: Evidence from Seattle." NBER Working Paper No. 23532, October 2017.

65   Cengiz, Doruk, Arindrajit Dube, Attila Lindner, and Ben Zipperer. "The Effect of Minimum Wages on the Total Number of Jobs: Evidence from the United States using a Bunching Estimator." Working Paper. April 30, 2017.

empowered to put more time and effort into a job. When workers are treated well and are paid well, they are more likely to do extra things to help out the business, such as picking up trash in the parking lot, straightening up tables and chairs, being nice to customers, and not wasting food and other materials.

Moreover, when the hourly wage is raised at a fast-food restaurant, such as McDonald's, it attracts workers who might not otherwise be in the labor force. The at-home parent who has some time to spare while their children are in school may decide to spend a few hours working at a nearby fast-food restaurant if the hourly pay makes it worth their while. The same may be true for retirees and students who have the time and may be willing to work for reasonable compensation. This can create a *crowding-out* problem for marginal workers, who may not have the social skills, reliability, and productivity of other workers who are now willing to work at the higher wage.

While there may be times when an individual business may step out of line and offer significantly higher wages than its competitors, as was the case of Henry Ford in the early days of the automobile industry, it is easier for businesses to make such changes when all of them do so at the same time. One fast-food restaurant may want to attract workers from other businesses paying somewhat higher wages but might be hesitant to raise its wages and prices unless nearby competing restaurants raise their wages and prices too.

The objective of a minimum wage increase is to increase money going to low-wage workers, but conservatives often object, saying that the minimum wage causes job loss and reduced working hours for these workers. Are they correct? Some solutions require that two tools be used simultaneously. For example, a bolt may go around and around, and not tighten when you try to screw it in with a screwdriver. The solution is to hold the nut with a pair of pliers while you screw in the bolt. Applying this analogy to the minimum wage discussion, we use two tools: combining the minimum wage (screwdriver) with an appropriate economic stimulus (pair of pliers) could provide just the right combination of tools to get more money into the hands of workers *without* net job loss or reduced total work hours for the economy as a whole.

Consequently, minimum wage laws can actually work to increase the flow of money to lower-income workers—as long as the increases are not excessive and are accompanied by a modest stimulus, such as Germany's work-time subsidy in which businesses are provided with some degree of government compensation to maintain jobs and work hours.

This is particularly important and useful when the economy is weak, such as in a recession, and needs an injection of consumer demand. Under the right conditions, the increased spending can overcome the higher-wage effect on employment and lead to higher employment rather than less employment. Combining a minimum wage increase with additional economic stimulus (e.g., infrastructure spending) when the economy has excess capacity can counter any negative employment effects of a modest minimum wage increase.

This stimulus effect will not work well and may in fact be counterproductive in the face of rapidly rising inflation when the economy is running at full capacity with low levels of unemployment. However, in recent years a combination of globalization providing an ever-widening supply chain and rapidly improving labor-saving technologies has greatly reduced the threat of runaway inflation.

EARNED INCOME TAX CREDIT OFFERS TARGETED SOLUTION

A more targeted approach to helping the working poor is the Earned Income Tax Credit (EITC). The EITC supplements the pay of workers who have low annual earnings, especially those with dependent children. It is both an earnings supplement and a work incentive combined. The requirements for 2019 included no more than $3,600 in investment income and limits on adjusted gross earnings of no more than around $15,570 to almost $56,000, depending on the number of qualifying dependent children in the household. Benefits ranged from $529 for earners under the age of 65 but older than 25 with no qualifying children, to over $6,557 for such earners with three or more qualifying children. The existence of the EITC provides an additional incentive for working, but that incentive declines as the person's income increases, and it stops completely once the appropriate earnings limit is reached. If the goal is to encourage labor force participation and increase the money flow to those in greatest need, the EITC is a useful and powerful tool that can appeal to those at both ends of the political spectrum.

MONOPOLIES CAUSE INEFFICIENT RESOURCE ALLOCATION

Monopolies and oligopolies are categories of industrial organization where one seller or just a few dominate and set prices higher than marginal costs, such that output is suppressed relative to a competitive market. The industry provides less output at higher prices and fails to achieve an efficient allocation of resources for the economy overall. Historical examples include Andrew Carnegie's US Steel Corporation, John D. Rockefeller's Standard Oil Company, and the American Tobacco Company. Carnegie and Rockefeller were ruthless in first undercutting their rivals' prices, next gobbling up their competitors for very little money, and then raising prices to sky-high levels once their competition was safely and completely gone. Later on, after much public criticism and, apparently, an accumulating sense of guilt and/or duty to the country,

Carnegie and Rockefeller established foundations to reflow some of their enormous wealth back into the economy.

Often the choice is between a service provided directly by the government or a private, regulated monopoly. Government operations are directly accountable to the public and can be more closely scrutinized by journalists from newspapers, television, and radio, as well as by individuals who report to their fellow bloggers and the public over social media.

Fiercely competitive businesses might offer greater efficiency in generating profits for their owners. But, as explained in any introductory economics textbook, monopolies generally do not result in efficient resource allocation. In particular, a monopoly does not provide the highest-quality product at the lowest-possible price. Resources are underutilized with less quantity than would be provided by competitive firms. Even a highly regulated monopoly demonstrates monetary leakage in the form of profits paid for by excess fees and/or taxes. Direct government control is sometimes a better option by providing better services at a lower price with greater accountability.

An example of a breakup of monopolies is that of American Telephone and Telegraph (AT&T), which was broken up into six companies that became known as the Baby Bells. As industries become more concentrated through mergers and acquisitions, pricing power is again emerging as an important economic issue. Google, Apple, Amazon, Facebook, and other technology companies have become so dominant in their respective domains that more antitrust action may be taken in the coming years in the United States and/or in Europe.

Similarly, monopsonies and oligopsonies are situations where one buyer or just a few face a large number of sellers and are able to set (or pay) prices lower than would be available under competitive conditions. Such a condition is not unusual; in fact, there's a natural tendency for companies to act as a labor monopsony (a single buyer of a particular type of labor) or a labor oligopsony (one of a limited number of buyers of a particular type of labor). In an ordinary market, excessively low prices significantly reduce the overall supply; in this case, however, resources are not allocated as efficiently as they normally would be. Some examples include tomatoes and coal. Historically, Heinz Company had a monopsony on buying tomatoes in Ontario, Canada. Similarly, local coal mines dominated towns in Appalachia, where other comparable employment opportunities were virtually nonexistent; in this case, coal companies in Appalachian towns had monopsonies on employment in coal production. In like manner, Amazon has oligopsony power in the retail book market, while Walmart has oligopsony power in the brick-and-mortar retail business generally. If your book is not available on Amazon or your retail product is not available in Walmart, then you are missing a large part of the market. How can these markets become more equalized? Improved communication, transportation, and immigration opportunities can help reduce the number of monopsonies and oligopsonies and restore efficient resource allocation.

Technically, banks are not monopolies or oligopolies, because there are so many of them. However, some banks are so large that they are a threat to the stability of our entire economy. In 1933, Congress passed the Glass-Steagall Act, which both separated commercial from investment banking and created the Federal Deposit Insurance Corporation (FDIC). However, in a flurry of deregulation legislation and in response to pressure from the banking industry to allow banks to make more profits, in 1999 Congress passed the Gramm-Leach-Bliley Act, which removed the restriction separating commercial from investment banking. This undermined the stability of our banking system by spreading the risks inherent in investment banking to commercial banking.

After 1999, banks took on unsustainable mortgage risk and, to make matters worse, bundled them into various financial derivative packages in an attempt to disguise their risky nature. This created a moral hazard incentive problem, because in addition to being too big to fail, the banks were still covered by the FDIC. The government-sponsored enterprises Fannie Mae and Freddie Mac also provided guarantees for the mortgages that they packaged into mortgage-backed securities. With this arrangement, any bad risks the banks took would be covered by the American taxpayers.

Today, in spite of a number of attempts to correct this problem, Bank of America, Bank of New York Mellon, Citigroup, Goldman Sachs, JP Morgan Chase, Morgan Stanley, State Street Bank, and Wells Fargo command such vast resources that any one of them could collapse—and take the whole economy down with it.

PATENTS, LICENSING, AND COPYRIGHTS

Some monopolies, such as those designated by our patent and copyright laws, were created by government to increase investment in new ideas and technologies. Patents and copyrights suppress competition in the short term to smooth out the risk-return curve over the long term. Pharmaceutical companies take years and spend lots of money trying to find a drug to cure a particular disease. Competing pharmaceutical companies could quickly copy the drug without paying the research and development costs. The first company would be unlikely to recoup its costs and would lose money overall if it were not for their drug patent preventing other drug companies from acting as free riders until the initial research and development costs had been paid off. If patents cover too short a period, the money flow is not adequate to reward the large initial investment required to create them. If patents are maintained for too long, on the other hand, competing investments and potential technological improvements are suppressed.

Occupational licensing in some professions is a way of enforcing barriers to entry and increase wages. About 29 percent of the labor force is licensed, corresponding with a commensurate increase in wages of about 18 percent.[66] In 1950, about 35 percent of the labor force was unionized while fewer than 5 percent were licensed. Now less than 7 percent of the labor force is unionized, but more than 29 percent are either licensed or government certified. The effect of unions was to reduce income inequality by raising the pay of less-educated workers. On the other hand, the effect of occupational licensing has been to increase income inequality by increasing the income of the most-educated workers, especially doctors and lawyers.

Clearly some licensing is needed to prevent scam artists from prescribing harmful drugs and therapies. However, of the 1,100 occupations that are licensed, fewer than 60 of them are licensed by all 50 states. Many types of licenses are required by less than a majority of the states. Large cities often add additional occupations to those that require licenses. The result is fewer job opportunities for many workers and higher prices for many services. The biggest problem is that the boards that determine the details on the licensing, including those tasks that cannot be performed without a license, are generally made up by those who already have a license and, therefore, have a vested interest in restricting competition and maintaining high prices for their services. These boards are generally subject to little or no independent oversight to protect the public interest.

Business necessarily operates within the confines of our democratic institutions with all of its rules and regulations. Not all of those rules and regulations are optimal. And some that were optimal may become

---

66   Kleiner, M. M., and Alan Krueger. "Analyzing the Extent and Influence of Occupational Licensing on the Labor Market." *Journal of Labor Economics*, Vol. 31, No. 2 (2013): S173–S202.

less than optimal as conditions change and new opportunities emerge. Establishing patent and copyright monopolies or licensing oligopolies might make sense to encourage investment and education in the short run, but in the long run they may suppress innovation if defined too broadly or maintained for too long.

SUMMARY, OVERVIEW, AND TRANSITION

The focus of this chapter has been on the central role of the government in establishing, policing, and maintaining the free enterprise system, with all the distortions, defects, and problems that the free market can engender. Efficient resource allocation has to take into account and adjust for positive and negative externalities, common property resources, monopolies, oligopolies, monopsonies, and oligopsonies, among other deviations from an imaginary world that automatically and perfectly adjusts to all supply shocks and demand shocks.

This chapter reviewed the role of government in imposing minimum wage laws, an Earned Income Tax Credit, patents, copyrights, and licensing. It also considered the distortions generated by asymptotic information in the marketplace. All these factors and considerations alter and divert the money flow, which can result in economic instability. The money flow paradigm mandates that government stay on top of all these considerations and circumstances to keep the economy on an even keel and not mistakenly rely on free enterprise to correct these problems that, without government intervention, would lead to inefficient resource allocation and economic instability.

The next chapter looks at the role that politics and special interests play in distorting the money flow. The results of political manipulations are partly determined by the different marginal propensities to consume, along with the demand multiplier and the velocity of money. Maintaining the proper money flow requires keeping track of all of these considerations and directing the money flow appropriately to compensate for these distortions.

CHAPTER 6

DISTORTED MONEY FLOW: TECHNOLOGY AND "PAY-TO-PLAY" POLITICS FAVOR CAPITAL, NOT LABOR

Income and wealth accumulate at the top of the income and wealth scales in part as a result of the transition from a largely variable-cost economy to a largely fixed-cost economy via automation. This results in directing more wealth to the owners of capital and relatively less wealth to workers, and such a distorted money flow can threaten the productivity and stability of an economy.

MULTIPLIER EFFECT AND VELOCITY OF MONEY

Printing more money by itself may not generate sufficient demand if the money just goes into the banking and financial system and does not go to those who would use it to purchase additional goods and services. It is not just a matter of how much money is in the economy but what is the rate of turnover—or velocity—of money at any given time. Money may turn over faster in some sectors of the economy than in others. Wealthy individuals using the money may increase the turnover in the ownership of real estate, paintings, and stocks and bonds without increasing the demand for goods and services. Money flowing to workers may result in a greater increase in demand for products and services, especially when their money goes directly or indirectly to other workers who also purchase more labor-intensive amenities. In a sense, my expenditures are your income, and your expenditures are my income.

The multiplier effect of any injection of money into the economy depends very much on where that money is injected and where it flows from there. Businesses earn higher profits from a more rapid turnover in money, as long as they are able to expand their production to accommodate the increase in demand. The same level of demand may be generated by a small amount of money turning over rapidly or a large amount of money turning over slowly. Of course, too much money turning over too rapidly could lead to inflation.

The threat of inflation has been reduced significantly by the rise of the internet and globalization. Easy access to additional goods and many services has been greatly enhanced by online ordering. While world sources are not inexhaustible, they do provide a new buffer to forestall the emergence of a sudden, rapid rise in inflation, especially in a free trade environment with greater communication and transportation efficiencies.

After World War II, extreme income inequality was avoided through government action and business restraint. Marginal tax rates were high, unions were strong, and the moneyed classes maintained a low profile while exhibiting a strong sense of duty to serve others, or at least to not blatantly flaunt their wealth and exploit others. But asking the owners of capital—those with the money—to rely on self-control alone is neither efficient nor sufficient for ensuring the well-being of the economy as a whole.

In his book *Capital in the 21st Century*,[67] Thomas Piketty presents extensive empirical evidence verifying the tendency for money to accumulate in the hands of the owners of capital.[68] This can be seen in the stagnant wage growth and declining real incomes of the middle class and the enormous fortunes accumulated by the very wealthiest investors. When a smaller and smaller portion of the money flow goes to labor and a larger and larger portion goes to capital, demand shrinks, and the economy slows or even slips into a recession—bringing with it high levels of unemployment. The "My America" Federal Reserve bank accounts (described in chapter 3) are designed to help alleviate such a scenario by adjusting the demand for goods and services to ensure full employment while maintaining a target level of inflation.

Politicians who are beholden to special interests and corporate executives who are shortsighted have always tried to block corrective

---

67 Piketty, Thomas. *Capital in the 21st Century*. Cambridge, MA: Harvard University Press, 2014.

68 Piketty showed that the average return to capital, r, is usually greater than the growth rate, g, of the economy for major developed countries (i.e., r > g). This is not contradicted by the fact that the economy's growth rate, g, exceeds the risk-free interest rate, i (i.e., g > i). However, it does suggest a disequilibrium condition where capital's marginal product per dollar of capital is greater than labor's marginal product per dollar of labor. This has been happening because technical change has been occurring faster than the economy can keep up. For example, I hadn't finished the process of replacing my incandescent light bulbs with the curly fluorescent light bulbs before the LED light bulbs came on the market. As more capital is employed, its marginal product falls, but this has not been occurring fast enough to settle into a long-run steady state equilibrium.

actions aimed to restore adequate money flow in our economy. In the next section, we will explore how distorted market power works to greatly overcompensate CEOs well above any solution that could plausibly be described as efficient resource allocation by natural competitive market forces.

CEO PAY AND THE REPRESENTATIVE AGENT PROBLEM

Market inefficiencies point to broader and more serious interference in our free market system. From the time when Locke's concept of private property was undermined by the divorcing of sweat equity from capital, the ownership of capital has become more and more separated from the control of capital. This problem is known in economics as the *representative agent problem*. This focuses on how the agent's (the CEO's) interests diverge from the interests of the owners. In particular, as Steven Clifford explained in his book *The CEO Pay Machine*, corporate boards often formulate CEO pay packages with narrow, short-term incentives that divert chief executives from the long-term development and success of their corporations.[69] CEO pay is not determined by some anonymous, independent, or efficient market mechanism but by a board *largely chosen by the CEO* and generally made up of other CEOs who already have a cordial relationship with the CEO—and who are, more often than not, a group of older white males. In "negotiations" with the board, the CEO has a pay-package consultant who specializes in maximizing the CEO's compensation package. Every board has an incentive to set a high standard for CEO pay so that when board members come up for review of their compensation to their companies, their fellow CEOs will also be generous with them.

---

69   Clifford, Steven. *The CEO Pay Machine*. New York: Penguin Random House, 2017.

The CEO pay package involves determining a peer group percentile ranking, compensation targets, performance measures, bonus ranges with bonus targets called bogeys, and equity awards, along with a generous "golden parachute" in case the whole thing doesn't quite work out. The board forms a compensation committee of insiders to work with a consulting firm that specializes in formulating CEO pay packages. The consulting company may have other business with the company in which key decisions are being made by that very same CEO.

The board also has an interest in projecting a positive image for the company, so they do not try to offer the middle-of-the-road, 50th-percentile ranking for their CEO's compensation, but something closer to the 75th percentile or above. This creates an upward bias to CEO pay as the whole range of comparable CEO peer-group pay spirals upward year after year.

The idea that the market will automatically correct such a fundamental flaw is naïve, and many corporations with different profit-maximizing or revenue-maximizing time horizons coexist for extended periods without any sort of automatic correction.

When ability and sweat equity are separated from ownership, all sorts of inefficiencies can arise and persevere, regardless of mistakenly labeling it as a "free market" system. In this case, not only are the workers and their sweat equity divorced from any ownership in the capital equipment and technology with which they work, but also the *representative agent* (CEO) often has interests that are somewhat different from the vast majority of the owners (stockholders) of the company.

When compensation boards are composed primarily of other friendly CEOs, exactly who is representing the interests of the owners who purchased the company's stock and the workers who did the work to produce the company's products? Why are unions striking for higher pay seen as disruptions of the efficient operation of free enterprise while this CEO pay process is often dismissed as the efficient working of supply and demand in an open, fair, and free market? Exactly how does this process efficiently match the supply and demand for CEOs? The current CEO pay process clearly does *not* represent the efficient allocation of resources in a free market. Quite the contrary, it is a significant and substantial market distortion.

But if it's wrong for CEOs to stick together to increase each other's pay, isn't it also wrong for workers to stick together by forming unions to raise their pay? The next section will address this issue.

DO UNIONS RESTRICT COMPETITION AND FREE ENTERPRISE?

One rule of free enterprise is that resource allocation can become distorted when one party gets too much power in selling products or services, such as in a monopoly, or in buying products or services, such as in a monopsony. Free enterprise works best when there is balanced and vigorous competition in every market.

As discussed in chapter 5, there is a natural tendency for companies to act as a labor monopsony (a single buyer of a particular type of labor) or a labor oligopsony (one of a limited number of buyers of a particular type of labor). Remember the coal miners in Appalachia. On the other hand, perfect competition assumes a *large* number of buyers and sellers of any particular type of labor service.[70]

---

70   For a discussion on the role of labor unions in maintaining a balanced and efficient allocation of resources in the face of a company's market power in competitive markets, see this 2018 EPI research paper: Bivens, Josh, Lawrence Mishel, and John Schmitt. *It's Not Just Monopoly and Monopsony: How Market Power Has Affected American Wages.* Washington, DC: Economic Policy Institute, April 2018.

To illustrate this, consider a hypothetical situation of a labor monopsony. Imagine an isolated town where the dominant employer is Walmart. But to make this interesting, let's assume that the five Walmart checkout counters compete with one another in the hiring of checkout clerks.

At first this works well. When one checkout lane offers too low a wage, it is shunned by potential employees who gravitate to a checkout lane offering a higher wage. By the same token, if a potential employee demands too high a wage, a checkout aisle will look for some other potential worker who is willing to work for a lower wage. The laws of supply and demand effectively and efficiently solve the resource allocation problem of determining the equilibrium wage rate and employing all those willing to work at that equilibrium rate. This becomes the wage for that job at all five checkouts.

For example, out of five workers, one is exactly at his or her indifference wage and would not work for a penny less. Meanwhile the employer is just willing to offer the fifth checkout lane job at the equilibrium wage and would not be willing to pay a penny more. This outcome maximizes employment and is optimal for the economy as a whole.[71]

But then a problem develops. The checkout aisles band together and decide to lower wages; they refuse to employ anyone at the equilibrium wage. Instead they set a wage rate lower than the equilibrium. The balance of power has shifted. But no other jobs are available in this small town, so most workers accept the new lower-wage rate, although some do not, and others cut back the number of hours they are willing to work. Of the five workers, one is an old guy who says, "Forget this. I would rather retire than work for pennies." In this hypothetical town, where

---

71 Consistent with each worker maximizing his or her utility function and each employer maximizing his or her profits within a perfectly competitive market.

Walmart has become a labor monopsony or oligopsony (if there are a few other employers), the wage rate is set too low and the quantity and quality of labor is reduced. Labor resources are no longer allocated efficiently; too many potential workers have opted out of the labor market.

Studies that focus solely on minimizing the unemployment rate—yet ignore the labor force participation rate—can be misleading. It may be a better use of a laborer's time to go out in the forest and shoot deer and pick berries than work for five dollars an hour. A low labor force participation rate may indicate wasted labor resources when jobs are lumped together in blocks even though workers bargain individually.

However, let's say the hypothetical Walmart workers band together and form a union. They demand that Walmart restore the old equilibrium wage rate. This restores the balance of power. The wage rate returns to its previous level, where labor resources are allocated efficiently. The old guy out picking berries comes back to work once that earlier equilibrium wage is restored. Technically the monopsony has not been broken up, but its market-distorting effects have been countered and efficient resource allocation is achieved nonetheless.[72]

Even in competitive markets, employers control blocks of jobs while each worker is on their own. It is a bit like being unaffiliated in a neighborhood with many competing gangs. The individual (jobless laborer) does not have much power, no matter how competitive the gangs (employers). Power is inherently unbalanced. Labor resources are wasted whenever jobs are lumped together in blocks and negotiated

---

72   This is a simple application of what economists call *the theory of the second best*, where when one market is out of equilibrium, the optimal solution is not for all other markets to be in equilibrium, but rather for a counterbalancing market to be out of equilibrium also. Unions are often justified under the theory of the second best.

as such. This is another example of asymmetry causing inefficient resource allocation.[73]

Every country has limited resources: water, land, iron ore—and of course labor. When 89 percent of all workers worked in farming, land was the most important resource. Now less than 2 percent work in farming, and education pays a premium. Yet there are worker shortages caused by the fall in birth rates in the United States in recent decades and the baby boomer generation now reaching retirement age. One way to combat this shortage is through immigration, and of course improving education among all prospective labor, especially the younger ones. In this way we can help sustain our national GDP and meet the Social Security and Medicare needs of our growing pool of retirees.

Let's turn now to examples of ways in which real players influence (and distort) the market as we explore how special interests use inappropriate power to distort the rules and regulations that govern the allocation of resources.

CITIZENS UNITED ENDORSES "PAY-TO-PLAY" POLITICS

In 2010 in its *Citizens United* decision, the Supreme Court reinterpreted our Constitution and went against the intentions of our Founding Fathers by changing our one-person-one-vote system to essentially a one-dollar-one-vote system by declaring that corporations were *people*. It also allowed political action committees (more widely known as PACs)

---

73   George Akerlof won the 2001 Nobel Prize in economics for revealing the market-distorting effects of asymmetric information, but asymmetric economic power can have market-distorting effects also.

to finance campaigns to promote or defeat candidates for political office throughout the United States.

In effect, these decisions transferred enormous power to wealthy individuals and corporations and fundamentally changed our form of government from a democracy to a plutocracy. One of the key ways that these special interests accomplish this is by having "captured" politicians insert specific lines into our tax code that are often referred to as *tax loopholes*.

When the political establishment is controlled by some of the wealthiest bankers, hedge fund managers, and energy moguls, economic policy tends to be shortsighted. In fact, directing a large portion of the money flow to the wealthiest families in the short run may in the long run tend to make those very same families less wealthy than they would otherwise be. A slowing or contracting economy is good for no one. Getting a relatively larger piece of a much smaller pie can mean getting less pie in absolute terms.

The reality is, if the rich want to accumulate more and more money, they must provide a corresponding amount of goods and services to the poor and middle class. Think of it this way: my expenditure is your income, and your expenditure is my income. By allowing more money to flow to the working class in the short run, the wealthy might gain even more wealth in the long run. This is the advantage of thinking in dynamic rather than strictly static terms. A healthy, balanced economy creates a win-win situation where everyone benefits.

Special interests use "pay-to-play" to influence politicians so as to promote policies that actually distort the economy by directing a larger portion of the money flow to themselves in the short run. Large campaign contributions have given special interests special access to politicians to change their thinking on key economic issues. This is known as *cognitive capture*, even in those cases where there is no clear quid pro quo.

TAX LOOPHOLES WORK WELL FOR THE SPECIAL INTERESTS

Over many years, special interests have been able to get politicians to insert lines known as *loopholes* into our tax code. These loopholes enable those entities to substantially reduce their tax payments or even avoid paying taxes altogether. In an application of James Buchanan's public choice theory, the benefits of a tax loophole are highly concentrated, while the costs are widely distributed so only the beneficiary of the loophole has any real incentive to exert political pressure to get it enacted into law. In other words, those hurt by the loophole aren't affected badly enough to bother complaining.

The 2017 tax law passed by Congress and signed by President Trump did little to simplify the tax code or eliminate any of the loopholes. Instead it raised the standard deduction to $24,000 so that fewer middle-class taxpayers would be itemizing their deductions. This was presented as simplifying the tax code so that middle-class taxpayers could complete their taxes on a "postcard."

One of the loopholes would be the 750-hour rule. Under the Internal Revenue Code (IRC-469), the 750-hour rule says that anyone who spends at least 750 hours in any given tax year on property management can depreciate their property on their taxes, making their "losses" fully deductible. Many Americans own property. But if you can't prove that you, or someone you employ, has spent at least 750 hours in a given tax year managing your property, then this loophole doesn't apply to you. However, if IRC-469 does apply and you own a $200 million property, and you depreciate over 25 years at 4 percent per year for property acquired after the Trump tax cut of December 2017, you can deduct $8 million on your taxes in a given year. Basically, this means that you pay little or no income tax. In reality, real estate has generally appreciated considerably over the years, instead of depreciating. Ironically, the greater the appreciation in a property's value, the more the developer can depreciate on their taxes. When you purchase a more expensive property, you end up paying more in taxes, but a property developer might pay less as a direct result of purchasing a property that has greatly appreciated in value prior to the purchase.

This and other such rules have been added to the tax code under "pay-to-play," where special interests have contributed to the reelection campaigns of politicians in return for adding a line to our tax code. It is precisely the tax loopholes that explain why President Trump does not want to release his tax returns. No doubt Trump has paid little or no taxes. But that alone would not motivate him to avoid tax return disclosure. In fact, he would probably be proud to show that he was "smart" enough to avoid paying taxes. Rather, he does not want the public to know about the specific tax loopholes that enable a wealthy person to pay little or no taxes.

President Trump doesn't want the 750-hour rule removed, because he can only serve for a maximum of eight years and will undoubtedly go back to property management when he ends his time as president. Also, *The New York Times* revealed that the president's son-in-law, Jared Kushner, has used IRC-469 to avoid paying almost all taxes at least from 2009 to 2016 and, perhaps, for many other years as well.[74] This is just one of the many rules designed to transfer the burden of paying taxes from the special interests to everyone else.

Another example of systematic tax avoidance by special interests involves the use of IRC-482 for transfer pricing. By creating a separate business in an overseas tax haven, a business with a well-known brand

---

74   Drucker, Jesse, and Emily Flitter. "Jared Kushner Paid No Federal Income Tax for Years, Documents Suggest." *The New York Times*. October 13, 2018. https://www.nytimes.com/2018/10/13/business/jared-kushner-taxes.html.

name can dramatically reduce its tax liability. As a hypothetical example, imagine that your company's brand name is "Sterling." You create a business in an offshore tax haven, which is known as a controlled foreign entity, and sell your brand name to that new business. Every time you use the brand name "Sterling," you pay your offshore business a royalty payment. This moves profits overseas by creating another "cost" for your home business that then can be used to offset revenues and lower your taxes.

Any business with a distinctive and well-known brand name can use this gimmick to virtually eliminate or substantially lower its taxes. It is hard for the IRS to determine the true free market value of such a brand name, so you can charge almost any value. A similar method of tax reduction or elimination is used by creating a separate tax haven company that sells unique inputs to your home company. This provides another way to transfer the tax burden from the wealthy to the middle class.

Tax deductions and credits can at first appear to benefit the middle class but ultimately primarily benefit the rich. For example, the mortgage-interest deduction sounds like a great way to help middle-class families afford to purchase their first family home. Of course, all persons who do not own a home are automatically excluded from this benefit, which immediately eliminates the poor, a significant portion of the middle class, and anyone who rents. More importantly, the mortgage-interest deduction can only be used by those who itemize their deductions. The standard deduction removes most middle-class taxpayers from that group. The more expensive the home purchased up to $1 million, the greater the benefit from the mortgage-interest deduction and the more likely the taxpayer will benefit from itemizing their deductions. In addition, up to $100,000 of interest paid on a home equity loan can be deducted on your tax return.

At the end of the day the mortgage-interest deduction turns out to be just another way in which the tax rules and regulations benefit the rich at the expense of middle-class taxpayers. It also encourages further concentration of homeownership in already densely populated areas by subsidizing the most expensive housing in the United States, which tends to be concentrated on the East and West Coasts. The mortgage-interest deduction is great for Wall Street bankers and Hollywood movie stars, but it doesn't do much for the rest of us.

The capital gains tax can lower the tax rate paid on long-term capital gains and dividends from stocks to as low as 15 percent. Of course, those who own the most stock get the most benefit. The wealthiest top 10 percent of Americans own 84 percent of all the stock, so wealthy taxpayers generally pay a lower tax rate than that faced by less-wealthy taxpayers.[75] For example, Warren Buffett claimed that in 2011 his overall tax rate of 17.4 percent was lower than any of the other members of his office staff—who presumably earn a lot less and own a lot less stock.

The carried-interest tax loophole applies to venture capitalists, hedge fund managers, and partners in private equity firms. Their salary is renamed "paid compensation" and is treated as a distribution of investment fund profits. As such, it is considered as capital gains and taxed at a much lower tax rate. At Bain Capital, Mitt Romney's pay was treated as carried interest, so he paid taxes at a much lower rate than most of the rest of us Americans.

The distortion of the rules and regulations that determine who pays and who benefits from government can be seen at the state level, as well as the national level. After serving on the economics faculty of the University of Notre Dame for thirty years, I retired and moved to Kansas City, Missouri, in 2005. On our first visit to the state capital in

---

75   Wolff, Edward N. "Household Wealth Trends in the United States, 1962 to 2016: Has Middle Class Wealth Recovered?" NBER Working Paper No. 24085, November 2017.

Jefferson City, my wife and I went to a restaurant near the Capitol for breakfast. Sitting near us were several men in conversation. Another man walked past and stopped to say to one of the men, "Good to see you, Senator," and briefly exchanged pleasantries. After a while some of the men left and only the senator and one man remained. From the conversation, it appeared that the man represented some business group. Before they got up to leave, we heard the man say to the senator, "You have been good to us, Senator, so we want to do something for you." He then handed the senator an envelope. We then understood why the interests of most regular people may not be so well represented. They fail to show up with envelopes.

1960 TRANSITION FROM ARISTOCRACY TO MERITOCRACY

The manipulation of our tax code has taken place over the last 20 years or so. It is a result of both shortsighted business interests and the emergence of the *nouveau riche*. Before 1960, America was ruled by an aristocracy. Legacy was the key to success in higher education and business. The elite were systematically separated from the rest of society. They attended separate schools from kindergarten through graduate school. I saw this firsthand. My mother was from a successful family from England. Her father planned and directed the laying of cable across the Atlantic and managed the telegraph traffic office in the financial district in New York City.

My mum developed tuberculosis when I was quite young. I was sent off to a British-style boarding school on the Hudson River in Nyack, New York, not far from the Tappan Zee Bridge and close to New York

City.[76] The father of one of my first roommates was president of a Latin American country, which was also ruled by a wealthy elite. I learned about income inequality early on as my 35-cents-per-week allowance paled in comparison with my roommate's $25 per week. After several years, I was sent off to The Lawrenceville School near Princeton, New Jersey, where I again found myself among highly well-to-do and privileged boys. However, at that time there was a strong sense of *noblesse oblige* among the wealthy East Coast families. Like President George W. Bush, many were "compassionate" conservatives. Generosity, perhaps motivated by privileged guilt, ruled the day. Taking an excessively large corporate salary was not considered proper. Until the 1960s, wealthy people were expected to hide their wealth, and most stayed out of politics and the public spotlight.

This continued until the system was partially dismantled starting around 1960 under the leadership of Harvard president James Bryant Conant and his assistant Henry Chauncey.[77] Before 1960, your high school grades and test scores were not as important as legacy, which included the private boarding school you had attended, and, more importantly, where your father, uncle, or grandfather had gone to college. My mother's family had Harvard roots, while my father's side was all Yale. With a good Ivy League diploma, graduates obtained corporate jobs through the old-boys system.

---

76   Nyack Boys School. It was an old Dutch mansion overlooking the Hudson River. It consisted of several magnificent stone buildings on beautiful grounds bordered by an extensive wooded area. In some ways, it resembled the infamous Hogwarts of Harry Potter fame, and even had a secret panel between the kitchen-storage area and the wood-paneled basement entertainment room. Later it was renamed Nyack Junior School to allow for the admission of girls.

77   For additional details and discussion: Brooks, David. *Bobos in Paradise*. New York: Simon and Shuster, 2000.

We like to call ourselves the "land of opportunity," but numerous studies have shown that America has had less upward mobility than most of the other developed countries in the world.[78] In other words, if you were born in a lower socioeconomic class in America, you are statistically less likely to move to the middle class or upper class than you would be in many other comparable countries. Unfortunately, statistical studies have shown that financial success in America is highly correlated with the education and income of our parents. Our system of financing public schools from local property taxes has ensured that children living in the poorest neighborhoods get the worst education. The limited number of exceptions doesn't refute the general rule that in America being born in a wealthy family with well-educated parents has traditionally given a child a tremendous advantage.

Around 1960, our system of higher education began to change with the introduction of the Scholastic Aptitude Test (SAT), the American College Testing Program (ACT), and other objective measures of an individual's potential college performance. In effect, the old aristocracy began to be replaced with something closer to a meritocracy.[79] College admissions officers began promoting a wider geographical distribution for incoming freshmen. Students at the Ivy League colleges began to represent a broader cross-section of America.

---

78   The statistics show that socioeconomic mobility is much greater in Canada, Finland, Norway, Denmark, and other developed countries than it is in the United States. See the evidence at https://www.epi.org/publication/usa-lags-peer-countries-mobility/.

79   A fascinating story of the distortion of this meritocracy can be found in Brill, Steven. *Tailspin: The People and Forces behind America's Fifty-Year Fall—And Those Trying to Reverse It.* New York: Penguin Random House, 2018.

GERRYMANDERING CREATES EXTREMISTS

The meritocracy continued until sometime in the 1980s when America started moving toward a new plutocracy, except without the restraining *noblesse oblige* mandate. As previously noted, the crowning jewel of the new wealth-based system was in 2010 with the *Citizens United* decision. When coupled with the gerrymandering of congressional districts, which help create the extreme partisan divide, political power shifted to serve the special interests that could afford to bankroll the increasingly expensive political campaigns required for reelection. Compromise became a dirty word in politics.

Gerrymandering is well known to result in representatives with especially extreme views who are unwilling to compromise with their congressional colleagues. To avoid having to deal with the increasing complexity of economic, social, and political issues, it became much easier to simplify things by taking an extreme position. By labeling their extremist views as their principles, some politicians just say that they don't debate their principles, as a way to avoid having to consider alternative points of view.

Restricting gerrymandering is challenging because congressional districts must represent approximately equal numbers of voters, and a method of restricting the shapes of gerrymandered districts is not yet in use. To devise such a system, one could simply start with the most compact possible district, which would be a perfect circle. The ratio of the circumference of a circle ($2\pi r$) to its area (πr^2) is easily calculated as $2/r$, where r is increased until the requisite number of voters is incorporated into the district. This ideal ratio can be used as a minimum value, which can serve as the basis for setting a moderately higher maximum legal value.[80] For every congressional district in the United States, the length of the boundary of that district could be calculated along with the area of that district, which can be obtained from county property tax records. A legal maximum limit could be placed on the boundary length divided by the area of the district.[81] A statistically interesting approach involves using Markov chain Monte Carlo techniques to determine how much a proposed district deviates from normal.[82]

This would establish a legal requirement that could substantially reduce gerrymandering and, hopefully, result in the election of congressional representatives who were less extreme in their political positions and more willing to find common ground with one another. And in economic terms, this would enable Congress to focus on working together to help ensure adequate money flow in a win-win strategy that would make us all better off than the current I-win-you-lose approach that now dominates partisan politics in Washington, DC.

---

80   Alternatively, a square having four sides, each with length l, has a boundary of $4l$, which captures an area of l^2.

81   The ratio of the boundary length or perimeter divided by the proposed district's area could be called the district's measure of concentration (DMC). A law specifying a maximum ratio (MR) for a given voter population could be set to make sure that congressional districts do not take on bizarre and inappropriate shapes. In other words, a plan specifying a district's boundaries would have to satisfy the relationship DMC < MR. Distortions deviating from a perfect circle could be allowed as long as the distortions don't produce a DMC higher than MR, where MR is a value to be set by law.

82   Duchin, Moon. "Geometry v. Gerrymandering." *Scientific American*, Vol. 319, No. 5 (November 2018): 49–53.

MAKE ELECTIONS FAIRER AND
MORE REPRESENTATIVE

Open primary elections would help select candidates who were less extreme and more willing to compromise. Allowing all voters to vote in each primary would be in the best interests of all voters and the nation generally. Some countries have replaced partisan primaries with one big primary election where the two candidates with the highest vote totals proceed to the general election.

Another method for reducing congressional partisanship would be to remove party affiliation from ballots in the general election so that voters would then be more inclined to learn the positions of each of the candidates. This has worked well in cities such as Kansas City, Missouri, where party affiliation has been removed for local elections. This, too, can serve to reduce the political influence of the special interests.

The Fair Representation Act proposed by Virginia congressman Don Beyer would combine congressional districts and set up elections for three to five representatives from each district under a ranked-choice voting system. This would eliminate the winner-take-all system of voting when applied to both primary and final elections.[83]

Currently, all the congressional representatives from Connecticut are Democrats, but 43 percent of the voters are Republican. Republicans from Connecticut get absolutely no representation in Congress. Similarly, Oklahoma is entirely represented by Republicans, but 32 percent of the voters in Oklahoma are Democrats. Oklahoma Democrats have no representatives in Congress.

When some states favor one party by narrow margins, while other

---

83   Additional details can be found at FairVote.org and https://ballotpedia.org/
Ranked-choice_voting_(RCV).

states favor the other party by wide margins, the narrow-margin states can capture a majority of seats in Congress with the votes of only a minority of the overall electorate.[84] Consider the vote: State 1 (Dems 5, Reps 4), State 2 (Dems 6, Reps 5), and State 3 (Dems 0, Reps 10). The Dems win a majority of the states, but the Reps have a majority of the votes (Dems 11, Reps 19). Congress then votes for policies that a majority of the people oppose.[85]

Ranked-choice voting in both primary and final elections would enable every voter's vote to count to some degree, even if their top choice was a relatively unpopular candidate. It would eliminate extremist, winner-take-all outcomes and allow more moderate candidates to get elected. The ranked-choice voting used in Maine eliminates the candidate who receives the fewest first-choice votes. The choices of those who chose that candidate are then shifted up one position so that their initial second choice becomes their first choice, et cetera.

The Supreme Court has failed to uphold the clear intention of the Founding Fathers in writing the United States Constitution by allowing *pledged delegates* as electors in the presidential selection process. The whole purpose of creating the Electoral College was to avoid a populist demigod from becoming president. The Founding Fathers intended to have an elected, but independent, board of electors make the final selection of the president of the United States after a great deal of discussion and debate. Freezing up this process by allowing pledged delegates clearly violates the intent of the Founding Fathers in writing the Constitution. To the extent that US Senate seats are counted in allocating Electoral College delegates, a citizen of Wyoming has more

---

84 This is a classic example of Simpson's Paradox.

85 For more on Simpson's Paradox, see https://www.researchgate.net/publication/273887620_Simpson's_Paradox_and_Causality.

than 68 times the voting power of a California voter. Not exactly one person, one vote! Delegates allocated by US House of Representatives seats are more representative.

Rather than attempting to restore the original intent of the founders, a more politically feasible solution is for each state to join the National Popular Vote Interstate Compact, in which each state agrees to assign all of its electoral votes to the candidate who gets the most popular votes in the fifty states and the District of Columbia. So far, the District of Columbia and the following ten states have signed this compact: California, Hawaii, Illinois, Maryland, Massachusetts, New Jersey, New York, Rhode Island, Vermont, and Washington. However, the compact only goes into effect once enough states representing a majority of electoral votes (270) have signed the compact. Otherwise, all states are free to follow their current procedures for allocating electoral votes. The signatories to the compact constitute 165 electoral votes, or 61.1 percent of the 270 needed for a majority.[86]

TAKE THE MONEY OUT OF POLITICS

Several measures have been proposed to reduce the influence of moneyed interests in politics. First, in light of the *Citizens United* decision, the Constitution needs to be amended to make it clear that only *human beings* are people and that corporations are not people.[87] Such an amendment

---

86   For a more complete discussion of the NPVIC, see the Wikipedia page: https://en.wikipedia.org/wiki/National_Popular_Vote_Interstate_Compact.

87   Steven Brill points out in his 2018 book, *Tailspin*, how deftly lawyers for the special interests were able to get the courts to consider corporations as people for this purpose, but to disassociate people (corporate leaders) from their corporations when those leaders oversaw the fraudulent and damaging practices that contributed to the 2008 recession.

would restore the financial limits on political campaign contributions that were removed in *Citizens United v. Federal Elections Commission* (2010) and *McCutcheon v. Federal Elections Commission* (2014). The enormous financial resources of the special interests could no longer drown out the voices of citizens of more modest means. This would be an important step in restoring the free speech of average Americans.

Second, Congress should pass the Anti-Corruption Act, which would prevent registered lobbyists from supplementing their lobbying activities with gifts to members of Congress. Registered lobbyists would also be forbidden to bundle contributions from a multitude of donors and then present those contributions to a member of Congress. Also, elected representatives and their senior staff would not be allowed to negotiate for high-paying lobbying jobs while in office or even taking such jobs for several years after leaving office. Elected officials would also be forbidden from fundraising activities during working hours when they are supposed to be working for their constituents. Other provisions of the Anti-Corruption Act require greater transparency in political fundraising and expenditures and removing barriers from voting.[88]

Third, the Securities and Exchange Commission, the Federal Elections Commission, the Federal Communication Commission, and other agencies and offices of the executive branch should be empowered to require transparency in political contributions from all publicly traded companies and government contractors.

---

88   For more on the Anti-Corruption Act, go to https://anticorruptionact.org/.

BEHAVIORAL ECONOMICS REVEALS IRRATIONAL DECISIONS

Wrong assumptions can result in poor economic policy. Economists who live in academia—far from the real world—used to dream of an economy with flexible wages and prices that would adjust automatically whenever an external supply or demand shock interrupted its path toward eternal material bliss. In an economy inhabited by rational, independent decision makers, these adjustments occur automatically as relative prices direct money flow according to the principles of supply and demand. Unfortunately, research in psychology and a relatively new area of study called behavioral economics have clearly demonstrated in carefully designed experiments that people are often neither rational nor independent in their decision-making.

Economic decisions have traditionally been viewed as based on a trade-off between time and money. However, a third factor now must be taken into account. Anyone familiar with behavioral economics in general, and the book *Nudge* by Richard Thaler and Cass Sunstein in particular, will appreciate that mental energy is also a major component in human decision-making.[89] Sometimes you have the time and money to do something, but you just don't have the mental energy to deal with it. In response to changing stock market conditions, you should adjust your stock portfolio, but you just don't have enough mental energy at the moment to get to it. Just sitting on the sofa and watching soap operas or old World War II documentaries seems a lot less mentally demanding.[90]

When faced with an economic (or any other) decision, the human brain typically does not recompute all possible courses of action using

---

89   Thaler, Richard H., and Cass R. Sunstein. *Nudge: Improving Decisions about Health, Wealth and Happiness*. New Haven, CT: Yale University Press, 2008.

90   Not to mention *Love It or List It, Aerial America*, or *Gilmore Girls*.

all available information (past and present), but instead relies heavily on stored templates. These templates are computed gradually over the course of a person's life experiences. A baby's brain works hard at differentiating between the behaviors of individual people and types of people (stereotyping) to save mental energy. While this is extremely efficient in saving mental energy, it can also lead one badly astray.

In politics and economics, platitudes are enhanced by alliteration, as well as short and simple logical chains. To some, Barry Goldwater's statement "Extremism in defense of liberty is no vice!" rings true. "The government that governs least, governs best" is another classic simplification, which is sometimes referred to as the "starve the beast" philosophy. Curtis LeMay offered, "If you kill enough of them, they stop fighting." Then there is Rush Limbaugh's "The world's biggest problem is the unequal distribution of capitalism." If he had instead said "the unequal distribution of capital," he would have at least better understood the money flow problem. Or Herbert Hoover, who said, "Blessed are the young, for they will inherit the national debt." All of these simple sayings are misleading in various ways. They both oversimplify these problems and ignore their dynamic aspects.

Another example would be in devising policies to raise the income of working-poor families whose breadwinners work hard but at jobs that do not pay enough to meet their basic needs for food and shelter. In some situations, raising the minimum wage will cause employers to cut back the hours of work and, thereby, the total incomes of the very employees the minimum wage is designed to help. But when combined with policies such as increased infrastructure expenditures, the positive spillover effects can accomplish the desired objective of raising the income of the working poor. As more money is spent on infrastructure, upping the demand for infrastructure workers, some workers will be drawn away from other occupations that pay less. This boost in income will inject more money into the economy as workers spend some of those dollars at fast-food restaurants and other places that pay their employees the minimum wage. This creates a win-win situation where the employer gets more business while the workers get a higher wage—without a reduction in hours worked.

MENTAL ENERGY PLAYS KEY ROLE IN ECONOMIC DECISIONS

Traditionally economists have tended to ignore anything that they could not measure. Once something becomes measurable, economists are quick to not only measure it, but also to create a market to buy and sell it. Mental energy in the form of electrolytes, oxygen, and calories consumed by the brain provides a measurable input that drives decision-making. Without mental energy there may not be enough time and money in the world to accomplish highly challenging mental tasks. Why pay lawyers by the hour when you could pay them by how much mental energy they are putting into your case? As neuroscience research advances, the role of mental energy will be much better understood.

With limited mental energy, people may be wary of other people whom they don't know and don't understand. Perhaps the biggest source of evil in this world is "us versus them." Policies are too often designed to help "good people like me" and not those "bad, undeserving people." The "others" are typically people of a different race, ethnicity, religion, or sexual preference. They may speak a different language or be from a different region. Our limited mental energy makes it difficult to understand or appreciate others who are different from us. In some communities, anyone showing concern for the "other" is dismissed as a "wannabe"—as in "black wannabe," "Muslim wannabe," or "gay wannabe." Economic policies based on stereotypes that assume that the "others" are all just welfare cheats do not help in establishing good money flow for a healthy economy. Removing these biases will improve money flow.

Distortions caused by economic policies that ignore the important role of mental energy in our economy need to be better understood. For example, people often follow the lead of others rather than use up their limited mental energy to think through each economic decision for themselves. This produces *contagion effects* where automatic adjustment to equilibrium comes about very slowly if at all. People often follow the lead of others in taking on too much debt and bidding up housing and stock prices beyond reasonable limits. When the stock market is "hot" and valuations are rising rapidly, everyone wants to get in on the action. Such collective exuberance leads to bubbles that ultimately burst. When I was growing up, my father, who spent 30 years as a stock analyst on Wall Street, used to say, "When the shoeshine boy starts offering you stock tips, it is time to get your money out of the stock market."

Over the years, this creates a pendulum effect in the stock market, and in debt markets generally. As investor enthusiasm grows, more and more people put whatever money they can get, including borrowed money, into the stock market. Investors buy more on margin by borrowing other investors' securities. This continues until the market reaches its limit where the excessive demand from the stock market bulls runs out. In recent years economists have come to call this a "Minsky moment," as discussed in chapter 2, named for Hyman Minsky, whose theories predicted such events. At that point in the market mania, the bears step in and the pendulum starts swinging back in the other direction. People exit the market in droves, often losing money in desperation to get out. Mass bankruptcies and widespread unemployment can occur. Readers of Nassim Nicholas Taleb's book *The Black Swan* will appreciate the likelihood of what under "normal" circumstances would be considered unlikely events.[91]

When these so-called unlikely events do occur, the government can play a critical role in providing additional stimulus to augment the automatic stabilizers that prevent the economy from falling too fast and too far.[92] The objective is not to punish those caught up in the irrational exuberance, but rather to get the economy back on track as quickly as possible. As Paul Krugman likes to say, economics is not a "morality play" but a real problem that requires reasonable and effective solutions.[93]

WEAK ECONOMIC DEMAND REFLECTS POOR MONEY FLOW

One aspect of the current economy that is not well understood is that the willingness of people to spend money on goods and services has slowed because of the aging of the population. Older people have always had a tendency to spend less on clothing and durables. As the baby boomers age, this tendency is having an impact on the economy. In the meantime, workers generally have seen little or no increase in their real disposable income. College debt now exceeds $1 trillion and is rising rapidly. With the little disposable money that they have left, younger people are choosing to spend a larger proportion of their incomes on experiences (often overseas) than on domestic goods and services.

The resulting chronic weakness in demand is one key factor that has

---

91   Taleb, Nassim Nicholas. *The Black Swan: The Impact of the Highly Improbable*. New York: Random House, 2010.

92   Taleb, Nassim Nicholas. *Antifragile: Things That Gain from Disorder*. New York: Random House, 2014.

93   Krugman, Paul. *End This Depression Now!* New York: W. W. Norton & Company, 2012.

caused the Federal Reserve Board to keep interest rates lower for a longer period of time than would otherwise be the case. With little or no inflation, there have been no significant cost-of-living adjustments for Social Security. These factors have kept the economy from expanding sufficiently without the help of monetary or fiscal stimulus.

When demand is strong, money turns over more quickly, and the bank accounts of both the wealthy and not-so-wealthy increase more rapidly. Again, the win-win economy wins by growing the pie, while the I-win-you-lose economy loses, where everyone is fighting for a bigger piece of the shrinking pie. When demand is weak, the wealthy can benefit themselves and everyone else by letting more money flow to the poor and middle class.

When demand is too strong and inflation threatens, we all collectively benefit by policies that slow demand and encourage businesses to invest in expanding their productive capacity. In other words, the direction of the money flow depends on the state of the economy. More money should go to consumers when demand is weak, while more money should go toward business investment when demand is too strong. The next section discusses the role played by the quantity and velocity of money in increasing or decreasing consumer demand.

QUANTITY AND VELOCITY OF MONEY

Both the amount of money and the velocity—rate of turnover—of money must be taken into account. The same amount of money passing through the economy more and more quickly could reach a rate of turnover that outstrips the economy's ability to supply that amount of goods and services in that short of a time period. Inflation can be caused by too much money chasing too few goods and services, or, conversely, by a smaller amount of money flowing too quickly through the economy.

Inflation may be held off temporarily by freeing up trade restrictions to allow more imports of goods and services to supplement our internal productive capacity where necessary.

It is in our national interest to not only keep our own workforce fully employed but also help maintain a healthy world economy. International money flows work best when we all work together in conjunction with the International Monetary Fund, which provides credit for economies in trouble, and the World Bank, which works to help the poorest and least advantaged people of the world.[94]

Just as blood flows through different parts of the body at different rates, the velocity of money varies as money works its way through the various paths and avenues of the economy. Increasing demand is not just a matter of dumping more money into the economy. For a healthy economy, the money must flow to all of the outer extremities and hidden corners of the economy (including struggling inner cities and rural Appalachia) to ensure full employment and strong economic growth. One cannot claim to have achieved efficient resource allocation if important resources (people) are left unemployed.

This does not mean that the target unemployment rate must be zero. A dynamic economy requires some turnover in jobs as workers move from industries that are out of date or out of favor with consumers into up-and-coming industries. Consequently, there will always

---

94   In place of the "us vs. them" attitude, we need to focus on the Rawlsian idea of working to help the "least advantaged." Anyone who understands and appreciates the win-win strategy can see how quickly we can grow the world's economic pie by helping to fight disease and poverty throughout the world. For maximum economic growth, the whole is always bigger than the sum of its parts. Working collectively in concert with one another will bring each of us greater economic well-being than focusing only on our own individual economic needs and desires. In his *Theory of Moral Sentiments*, Adam Smith emphasized the need to help the poor in order to help maximize the wealth of nations.

be some frictional unemployment—a temporary situation, as workers change jobs.

There is much debate among economists about what is the non-accelerating inflation rate of unemployment (NAIRU). Achieving an unemployment rate below the NAIRU could lead to an unacceptably high rate of inflation, while obtaining a rate above the NAIRU leaves "money on the table" with regard to efficient resource allocation. The Federal Reserve System's Federal Open Market Committee is especially interested in accurately determining the NAIRU as the basis for setting interest rates and other aspects of monetary policy. Professor Olivier Blanchard of MIT has provided an important analysis of the evidence of the potential impact, if any, of monetary policy on the NAIRU and related issues.[95]

A few people believe that a damaged or diseased body can always heal itself. They have a religious commitment to natural healing and avoid doctors. Most people understand that a doctor with knowledge of the latest research can help a person recover much more quickly. Doctors are now beginning to be assisted by algorithms that search the medical literature and offer judgments about appropriate diagnoses and protocols. Similarly, better forecasting with more efficient statistical artificial intelligence algorithms and the right economic policies can restore a proper balance in the money flow more readily than waiting for the economy to heal itself.

---

95   Blanchard, Olivier. "Should We Reject the Natural Rate Hypothesis?" Peterson Institute for International Economics and Massachusetts Institute of Technology. November 21, 2017. Version 2.0. https://www.aeaweb.org/conference/2018/preliminary/paper/sNyeNDdY.

TAXES AFFECT MONEY FLOW

The money flow associated with income inequality is dependent on, to a significant degree, the structure of the tax system. In some regions, especially in the South, there has been a "Fair Tax" movement to replace income taxes with sales taxes. Some states, such as Florida, have dropped income taxes in favor of sales taxes and property taxes. Sales taxes are especially regressive in that they place a higher burden of taxation on the poor. Sales taxes only apply to physical goods and services, but not to financial products such as certificates of deposit or stocks and bonds. Nor do sales taxes apply to the purchase of real estate in most cases. Since buying and selling expensive paintings,[96] real estate, and stocks and bonds often involves little, if any, sales tax, the purpose of the Fair Tax is simply to eliminate the income taxes paid by the rich and transfer the burden of taxation onto the poor and middle class via an increase in sales taxes. Why is there a sales tax on the goods and services purchased by the lower and middle classes but no sales tax on financial products such as the certificates of deposit or stocks and bonds purchased by the wealthy? Shouldn't a Fair Tax include all that we buy? To be fair, a Fair Tax should be applied to financial products too.

As income inequality grows, more and more wealth accumulates in the hands of fewer and fewer people. This has a big impact on the path that money takes through the economy. The money flow is altered when the rules of the game are changed. Money going to pay taxes cannot be used by those paying the taxes to buy more goods and services. In fact, higher sales taxes discourage people from buying more goods and

---

96   To avoid sales tax on expensive paintings, use a "1031 exchange," which allows people to buy and sell artwork with little or no sales tax.

services. During a recession, changing the rules of the game to give rich people more money at the expense of poor and middle-class people does not help in the effort to restore full employment. Just as extreme equality of incomes and wealth can inhibit economic growth, extreme inequality can also reduce growth. Maximum growth is achieved at an intermediate level somewhere between the two extremes.[97] When the economy remains depressed, it is not just the poor and middle class who suffer. The rich are also losing out on the benefits of a dynamic, growing economy. Ironically, if the rich are willing to take a larger share of the burden in the short run, they may end up with greater wealth in the long run by virtue of a healthier economy.

MISCONCEPTION IN ECON 101

A major misconception comes from taking introductory economics, often called "Principles of Economics," at your beloved college or university. While the concepts presented there are important for understanding how equilibrium prices and quantities are determined in an ideal setting, there is little or no explanation of how exactly the shape of the supply and demand curves are determined. The answer requires moving from the simple, ideal world of introductory economics into the real world of laws and regulations that set the rules of the game for all participants. What are the labor laws? Are there restrictions on pollution? Who pays the taxes? How are imports and exports regulated? Why do special-interest groups have so much influence over the particular laws that benefit them? What limits are set on patents and

97 For an excellent review and analysis of the optimal level of inequality, read Ostry, Jonathan D., Prakash Loungani, and Andrew Berg. *Confronting Inequality: How Societies Can Choose Inclusive Growth*. New York: Columbia University Press, January 2019.

copyrights? What licenses and/or certifications are required to participate in certain professions such as hairdressers, cab drivers, florists, doctors, and lawyers?

If you understand the system and how the rules are set, you may be able to game the system. Otherwise, you are just left to the mercy of the laws of supply and demand. The rules are set to benefit the winner. If you don't have much money in your checking account, you probably are going to have to pay for your checks. If you deposit more than some substantial amount, your checks might be provided for free. If you are not an accredited and active investor with more than a million dollars in investable funds, you probably have to pay a transaction fee when you buy or sell stocks and bonds.

The rules are set up to benefit the winner. We are led to believe in Econ 101 that the equilibrium outcomes are natural and cannot and should not be changed. Meanwhile, the special-interest groups are busy getting everything rigged in their favor behind the scenes. It is illegal to pay someone for their vote but not illegal to pay someone to ask for someone else's vote. We like to believe that we are all playing on a level playing field, and we hide behind a thin veneer of democracy. But in the end, the big guy gets what he wants.

MONEY FLOW IN A FREE MARKET

A key aspect of money flow is in understanding where the free market forces of supply and demand come from. They do not suddenly appear out of nowhere like the Holy Spirit. They emanate from the social and political environment. It is only in that context that freedom has any real meaning. Remember the example used earlier and think of yourself as a cave dweller in prehistoric times. If you have a chicken, it is the big guy's chicken. The big guy is free to take your chicken. If you have a pear tree, the big guy is free to take your pears. The only way you can be free is by making the big guy less free. Freedom is always a balancing act. My freedom to pollute the air curtails your freedom to breathe. Your wild and reckless driving puts my life and those of my loved ones at risk. Stop signs and traffic lights curtail my freedom while protecting your right to life, liberty, and the pursuit of happiness.

One important aspect of freedom is in the rules for dealing with asymmetric information where one side in a transaction has more knowledge about the product being traded than the other side. Examples include the market for used cars, where the seller has more knowledge than the buyer, or the market for insurance, where individuals have more knowledge about their own health than the insurance company. Consequently, in such markets the uncertainty causes prices to be distorted and resources to be allocated less efficiently than in the absence of the added risk. Asymmetric knowledge introduces uncertainty and risk, which causes used cars on average to sell for less and insurance to generally cost more.

Transparent pricing of well-defined goods and services allows for efficient exchange of resources to the benefit of everyone, as Adam Smith explained in *The Wealth of Nations*. Rules are established to prevent asymmetry, such as those forbidding the insider trading of stocks. Government standards are set to require revealing the ingredients of foods and beverages. Distortions occur when people have unequal access to essential market information. When snake-oil salesmen lie, we are fooled and misled into making inefficient decisions that do not maximize our overall well-being.

Adam Smith did not condone the market behavior of snake-oil salesmen or any other form of free market distortions. The free market Smith was referring to was not the one where the big guy is free to take your chicken. The government replaced the freedom of the big guy with a more egalitarian freedom established by a set of rules designed to benefit everyone to some degree—the key part of that sentence being "to some degree." Each segment of society may be affected differently by the free market rules that the government establishes. These rules are changed frequently through legislation, court rulings, executive decrees, and administrative regulations set by a wide assortment of local, state, and federal bureaus and agencies. The free market is defined by the combined effect of these forces.

The government does not "intrude" on the free market. The government defines, creates, and maintains the free market. Even the currency used to execute transactions in the free market is provided by government. Americans have lost sight of all this. The special interests that have the most influence over our government and the rules that it has established have encouraged us to think of the free market as a set of natural and indisputable laws that we must all accept as inevitable. Promoting the idea that a free market could exist apart from government usurps the debate about what the rules that define the free market should be.

The special interests know that they stand to gain the most from maintaining the fiction that government is somehow interfering with the efficient and natural functioning of the free market. Market failure exists in the form of monopolies and oligopolies, as well as positive and negative externalities. These inefficiencies often occur in the absence of specific rules and regulations, but sometimes as a result of such rules and regulations, as in the case of patents and copyrights. The rules can be set up to maximize market efficiency to overcome market failure, or they can introduce market failure where it did not previously exist. The efficient allocation of resources is about what set of rules is established by the government and not about whether or not government has a role to play in a free market.

MONEY FLOW AND LABOR
MARKET PRODUCTIVITY

Opportunity cost and productivity are key to money flow. At lower wages the quantity demanded of labor is higher, but the quality of labor is lower. Low labor quality means lower productivity. People often have alternatives in the nonwage sector. Elderly baby boomers may enjoy babysitting for the grandkids. College students may spend more time studying or playing online games. At-home parents may remain there even when the kids are busy in school if the prevailing wage is too low. At low wages, McDonald's may find workers who are unreliable and unproductive, quarrelsome with others, rude to customers—and either show up late for work or do not show up at all. Lowering wages is not the panacea that it is often touted to be. Efficiency wages offer wages above the market-clearing wage, which is the wage needed to attract job candidates with equal or better labor market qualifications.

But what if the job involves knowledge that has to be learned on the job over a longer period of time? In that case it may be in the employer's interest to pay the current jobholder a higher wage than the market-clearing wage. This creates a situation where the number of jobs for workers with a specific set of qualifications is too low at that higher wage to employ the number of workers available. Unemployment persists because these "overqualified" workers can't get work in their specific fields. This in turn creates involuntary unemployment that persists because firms are not willing to lower their wages for fear of losing their long-term employees—hardworking employees who have acquired the *additional* job-specific knowledge that has enhanced their productivity beyond what their unemployed counterparts could offer (because those counterparts haven't had the opportunity for on-the-job learning). It's a sort of catch-22, and such unemployment does not go away with time.

Using the example just described, here's an analogy: it is as if your car is running smoothly at 35 miles per hour (mph), but you really need it to be running at 65 mph. At such times government needs to intervene to stimulate the economy and increase employment beyond the suboptimal level set by the free market economy. Once the 65 mph level of employment is reached, the government can then back off and let the free market economy take over once again. Both politically and economically it is unacceptable for the economy to be left in a suboptimal equilibrium where there is a high level of unemployment resulting from the setting of efficiency wages that are too high for the employment market to clear automatically on its own.

To maximize the economy's potential, high-quality workers need to be enticed to enter the workforce. When wages are too low, workers do not earn enough to buy enough goods and services to keep the economy running at full steam. Employers do not make the profits they would have made if the economy were growing at its maximum potential. Most individual businesses are not large enough to have a substantial impact on their own. Raising wages may help attract better employees, but that increase in wages is dissipated over many other sources of goods and services, so overall demand does not increase sufficiently to bring the economy up to its full potential. A larger, more sustained increase in demand may be needed when the economy is particularly weak. As more and more workers reach retirement age, we need to ensure that the remaining workers are fully employed to sustain our national GDP and meet the increasing needs of our population, including our ever-increasing pool of retirees.

OLD INFLATION-BASED CYCLE REPLACED BY TRIPLE BUBBLE ECONOMY

During the 1960s, '70s, and '80s, our economy experienced business cycles with rising inflation countered by rapid interest rate increases by the Federal Reserve. Slow technical change, high levels of unionization, and a relatively low degree of globalization allowed wages and prices to rise quickly as our economy approached maximum capacity utilization. Once inflation was moderated and the economy slowed, the Fed injected more money back into the economy to bring interest rates back down, in an effort to encourage investment and employment.

However, as early as the 1990s, a new form of business cycle emerged to replace the previously prevailing one. With higher levels of globalization, low levels of unionization, and more rapid technological change, the new business cycle exhibited rising credit and stock market bubbles, replacing price and wage inflation as the source of economic instability.

Extreme inequality in income and wealth has led to a strange mix of huge amounts of savings owned by very few people—with most people living paycheck to paycheck while building up more and more debt. Motor vehicle debt and mortgage debt have been piled onto credit card debt and student loan debt. High and often unexpected medical costs have added even more debt. For more details, read Elizabeth Warren's book on the buildup of middle-class debt.[98] All this debt creates the first bubble, which is known as the *consumer debt bubble*. Without receiving adequate money flow, consumers are inevitably driven deep into debt. The consumer debt bubble just grows larger and larger over time. Such an economy is unsustainable. For further discussion of debt leveraging and monetary policy, read the incisive book *Debts, Deficits and Dilemmas*.[99]

---

98   Warren, Elizabeth, and Amelia Warren Tyagi. *Two-Income Trap: Why Middle-Class Parents Are Still Going Broke.* New York: Basic Books, 2003 (updated in 2016). Or listen to a summary of their data analysis and presentation of the evidence at https://www.youtube.com/watch?v=akVL7QY0S8A.

99   Beddoes, Zanny Minton, et al. *Debts, Deficits and Dilemmas.* London: Profile Books, Ltd., 2014.

Approximately 70 percent of our economy is accounted for by consumer expenditures. Consequently, strong consumer demand for goods and services is essential for stability and full capacity utilization. When consumer demand is inadequate, investment expenditures must make up the difference until consumer demand can be restored. Money flowing into savings must flow into investment to make up for the shortfall in consumer demand. To get businesses to invest more, interest rates must be lowered until all the savings are fully employed. But the pool of savings is too large. As mentioned previously, as wealthy individuals accrue more money, they buy more stocks, bonds, expensive paintings, and exclusive real estate, driving up prices to higher and higher levels.

The vast amounts of money flowing into savings drive real interest rates down to zero. No one is going to want to pay you to borrow their money. If I have one hundred dollars in savings, I might be willing to accept two dollars or even one dollar to loan it to you for a year. But don't ask me to *pay* you a dollar for the privilege of loaning you my money for a year. Consequently, much of the savings pile up and are not put to use as investment expenditures. As previously noted, this is known to economists as the Keynesian liquidity trap.

Money flows to the savings of large corporations and wealthy individuals rather than to lower- and middle-class consumers who would actually use the money to buy goods and services. When enormous amounts of savings build up, the Keynesian liquidity trap is inevitable. This creates the second bubble, which is the *wealthy-savings bubble*.

As corporations get more money, they often use it to buy back their stock rather than add more plant and equipment when consumers are unable to come up with the money to buy more goods and services. Stock market prices rise higher and higher as wealthy individuals and corporations buy more and more stock.

Then comes the third bubble: the *federal debt bubble*. Strapped for cash, the indebted middle class cannot buy back the goods and services it creates, so politicians step in with unpaid-for tax cuts and deficit spending to make up the difference and produce an ever-increasing federal debt bubble.

The extreme nature of this triple-bubble economy is relatively new in that it emerged starting in the 1990s. The old inflation in wages, as well as in goods and services, was gone. The money now flows into the financial markets to inflate stock prices but does not trickle down to the middle or working classes. The Federal Reserve's policy tools become inadequate. The wealthy-savings bubble has inflated both stock and bond prices while driving down interest rates to very low levels. The Fed finds that when recession threatens, its usual policy tool of buying Treasury securities in the New York financial markets to stimulate the economy by lowering interest rates is ineffective because rates are already abnormally low as a result of the wealthy-savings bubble. At the same time, the middle and working classes become unable to make their loan payments and the consumer debt bubble bursts as employers cut back working hours and lay off workers. The executive branch and Congress respond by driving up the federal debt bubble even more with unpaid-for tax cuts and federal stimulus expenditures.

SUMMARY, OVERVIEW, AND TRANSITION

This chapter focused on how special interests distort the money flow and contribute to economic instability. From bloated CEO pay to tax loopholes and gerrymandering, distortions redirect the money flow to create a permanent Keynesian liquidity trap with a consumer debt bubble, a wealthy-savings bubble, and a federal debt bubble. This encourages partisanship and

continued

political turmoil and creates long-term economic instability. In response to past economic downturns, the Federal Reserve has used its New York office to purchase Treasury securities to inject money into the financial markets and drive down interest rates. Although after a bit of a lag this may enable some money to trickle down and stimulate demand, the money flow paradigm rejects this approach as inefficient and contributing to long-term instability by encouraging more, rather than less, indebtedness.

Instead of injecting a large amount of money in this "pushing on a string" approach, the money flow paradigm calls for the creation of "My America" Federal Reserve Bank accounts, as discussed in previous chapters. Money injected into the financial markets tends to stay in the financial markets (pushing up stock prices), but money given directly to consumers tends to increase demand for goods and services immediately, requiring less money to attain a noninflationary target level for unemployment via the demand for goods and services.

The next chapter will focus on macroeconomic policies designed to deal with these money flow distortions. The ultimate goal is to develop the policy tools needed for government to secure a stable and healthy economy for everyone while achieving more efficient resource allocation.

CHAPTER 7

MACROECONOMIC POLICY: AUTOMATIC STABILIZERS, DEBT, AND THE ECONOMIC DEATH SPIRAL

For thousands of years, *Homo sapiens* managed to survive through good times and bad, through floods and droughts, and through scorching desert heat and icy-cold winters by planning ahead, preparing in advance, and adjusting their strategies as conditions changed. Politicians on either side of the aisle fail to grasp this when they opt for simple, shortsighted "solutions" that make for good sound bites but do not address the fundamental problems we face. This is especially important in current times as we go from the irrational exuberance of a booming economy on the brink of hyperinflation to a deep recession with high unemployment followed by a very slow recovery. We must strengthen, not weaken, our automatic stabilizers and give more authority, not less, to the professional economists who run our Federal Reserve Board. Relying on politicians to formulate timely and effective economic policy and to get the money flow right is unrealistic and a recipe for dysfunction and disaster.

FISCALLY PRUDENT USE OF MONEY FLOW

One common view of the economy is that nations, like families, should be fiscally prudent. We should balance our budgets so that our outflows exactly match our inflows. Some people claim that the government should act like any responsible family. They claim that a responsible and prudent family will always balance its budget. It will make sure that its expenditures always exactly match its income. But this is not what a prudent family actually does. A prudent family will not match its inflows to its outflows. When times are good, a prudent and responsible family will save money. It will save some of its income in anticipation of tough times.

When a recession strikes and the family breadwinners lose their jobs or prices rise suddenly, the prudent and responsible family will be able to get money from their savings account (deficit spending) to keep the family expenditures on an even keel. The family will be able to continue to put food on the table, pay their mortgage, and cover their children's needs. It won't be necessary to move to a cheap apartment, withdraw the children from extracurricular activities, skip the holiday presents, and cut back on clothing and food expenditures—while at the same time cutting back on nonessential expenditures. As long as the recession doesn't last too long, the prudent family can get by without major adjustments until the breadwinners find new jobs in a revived economy.

Government is in a similar situation. In good times it is not sufficient to balance a government's budget. Savings are essential. When the economy is running on all cylinders, economy-wide tax cuts are not appropriate. That is the time to pay off debt and avoid overheating the economy. Fiscal conservatives recognize that this would not be an appropriate time for tax cuts to pay off the special interests for their political campaign contributions. When unemployment is low and the economy is running at full capacity, that's the time to run a budget surplus and pay down the national debt. Unfortunately, running a budget surplus is politically unrealistic. Perhaps at the federal level we can only hope to avoid *not* adding to the debt when times are good and being willing to run a deficit just large enough to get the economy back on track when the economy is in a recession.

If a city has no savings account, and revenues dry up during a recession, the city will have no choice but to lay off teachers, firefighters, and police. Farsighted states and localities will follow the prudent family's example. Several states, from Alaska to Texas, have "rainy day" funds. When a recession strikes, they do not have to lay off teachers, firefighters, and police officers. They simply withdraw money from their "rainy day" fund until the crisis has passed. Some cities, such as Kansas City, Missouri, have reserve funds for this purpose. Even my neighborhood homeowners' association has a reserve fund to smooth out payments for snow removal, because the snowfall varies so dramatically from winter to winter.

It would be foolish to think that good times will last forever. While each economic crisis is in some way unique, we cannot expect the economy to maintain full employment and run at full capacity from now until eternity. Every family, locality, state, and nation should prepare itself for the next economic downturn. The bad news is that when a recession strikes, everyone suddenly saving more in anticipation of job loss or reduced incomes just makes matters worse. As explained in the next section, microeconomic incentives can sometimes systematically harm, not help, in reviving the economy.

DON'T DESTROY OUR AUTOMATIC STABILIZERS

Economists have long recognized that what works as an incentive and improves welfare in a person's micro economy can sometimes have the opposite effect in the macro economy. In the typical introductory economics course ("Principles of Economics"), we explain the *paradox of thrift*, where in a recession each family cuts back on expenditures out of fear of the family breadwinners losing their jobs. Ironically, each family's attempt to save more at the micro level contributes to a cutback in the demand for goods and services at the macro level, causing additional layoffs and a downward spiral that ultimately results in a reduction (rather than an increase) in total national savings.

Economists have come to understand that the assumption that people are independent decision makers who ignore what others are doing is fundamentally incorrect. People act in concert with one another either intentionally or unintentionally. They warn their neighbors about layoffs at local businesses and try to reduce or even minimize their expenditures at such times accordingly. Ant colonies and birds in flight are not the only ones who act in unison. Humans do it too. Pretending that contagion effects are not common ignores economic history in its entirety.

It is ironic that doing the right thing at the micro level can cause significant damage at the macro level. Families are right to save more when times are tough, but politicians are wrong to ignore the aggregate impact of such behavior on the overall economy. You don't have to do a lot of complicated mathematics to understand the need for action to counter contagion effects.

Automatic stabilizers help keep demand from falling too abruptly so that more people can keep their jobs and so that government revenues at all levels do not fall off a cliff.[100] The primary automatic stabilizers include unemployment insurance, food stamps, Medicaid, the Children's Health Insurance Program (widely known as CHIP), and other such programs specifically designed to help people who have been thrown out of work or are otherwise unable to support themselves and their families through no fault of their own. When the economy goes south, these programs help maintain essential demand to keep other people employed and stop the downward spiral.

Another automatic stabilizer is the progressive nature of our income tax schedule.[101] Under our tax structure, when incomes fall, the amount owed in taxes falls more quickly. This helps keep demand for goods and services from falling too abruptly. Automatic stabilizers have been weakened in recent decades as companies have shifted from reliable defined-benefit retirement pension plans to variable defined-contribution plans, which produce retirement accounts that tend to rise and fall with the stock market. This not only transfers risk from employer to employees, but it also contributes to the instability of the economy. There are also more temporary and part-time workers.[102] Such workers are typically not eligible for company retirement plans and end up relying solely on Social Security and Medicare. Along with contract workers, these workers comprise almost 20 percent of today's workforce.

100   McKay, Alisdair, and Ricardo Reis. "The Role of Automatic Stabilizers in the US Business Cycle." *Econometrica*, Vol. 84, No. 1 (2013): 141–194.

101   Auerbach, Alan J., and Daniel Feenberg. "The Significance of Federal Taxes as Automatic Stabilizers." *Journal of Economic Perspectives*, Vol. 14, No. 3 (2000): 37–56.

102   Biewen, Martin, Bernd Fitzenberger, and Jakob de Lazzer. "The Role of Employment Interruptions and Part-Time Work for the Rise in Wage Inequality." *IZA Journal of Labor Economics*, Vol. 7, No. 1 (2018): 1–34.

Setting aside the debate about whether we should be helping people in distress, a healthy economy requires that we prevent a substantial drop in revenues at all levels of government that would throw millions of government workers out of work, which in turn would cause a dramatic drop in demand for goods and services and result in layoffs in private businesses throughout the economy.

A balanced budget amendment to the Constitution of the United States would forbid deficit spending, prevent the activation and expansion of safety net measures, effectively destroy many of our automatic stabilizers, and substantially deepen and lengthen economic downturns. Without the automatic stabilizers, instead of a recession with about 10 percent unemployment, we might well end up with a full-blown depression with 25 to 30 percent unemployment. A balanced budget amendment is an exceptionally bad idea based on static instead of dynamic analysis.

DEBT OR ECONOMIC DEATH SPIRAL

The concepts of money, nations, and corporations owe their existence to our creative imaginations. As Yuval Noah Harari[103] has pointed out, *Homo sapiens* gained superiority over other humans and animals through their ability to create common myths, or what Nobel Prize winner Daniel Kahneman[104] calls "heuristics." These commonly shared rules of thumb or mantras control our day-to-day existence much more than we realize. Misguided, shared beliefs, such as the sun revolving around the earth, the

---

103   Harari, Yuval Noah. *Sapiens*. Tel Aviv: Kinneret, Zmora-Bitan, Dvir., 2011. Harari, Yuval Noah. *Homo Deus*. New York: HarperCollins, 2016.

104   Kahneman, Daniel. *Thinking Fast and Slow*. New York: Farrar, Straus & Giroux, 2011.

efficacy of trickle-down economics, or the denial of human involvement in climate change can lead us astray for generations.[105]

Many of our economic institutions and economic policies follow the economic theories of deceased economists. The idea that "you cannot solve a debt problem by adding more debt" is a nice-sounding heuristic, but it mixes apples with oranges when it confuses private debt at the micro level with public debt at the macro level. Adding public austerity to private austerity does not create prosperity, but rather a downward spiral leading to even greater debt and more austerity.

As noted in earlier chapters, a nation in an economic downturn is like a car moving slowly at 35 mph. When entering a highway, to increase the speed of a car traveling at 35 to a speed of 65 mph, we have to step on the gas. Once that injection of gas has brought us up to 65, it doesn't take that much gas to just cruise along at that same speed. We are better off taking action to restore the health of our economy in the short run than prolonging a recession to wait for recovery. A longer recovery means less productivity in the long run.

Ironically, when a recession develops, running a budget deficit in the short term can get us back on track more quickly and enable us to reduce our long-term debt. An economy running at full speed will always be more productive and generate more revenues than one held back by our reluctance to act decisively to bring our economy out of a recession.[106]

---

105   For a wider discussion of the role of misguided beliefs in economics, see Shiller, Robert. *Narrative Economics: How Stories Go Viral and Drive Major Economic Events.* Princeton, NJ: Princeton University Press, 2019.

106   See Paul Krugman's commentary that discusses these issues in more detail at http://www.economicshelp.org/blog/5342/books/end-this-depression-now-review/.

FEDERAL RESERVE POLICY
PREVENTS HIGH INFLATION

It is certainly true that issuing too much currency can undermine that currency's value. However, when the US Treasury sells Treasury bills, bonds, and notes in the New York treasury market in return for cash, and the Federal Reserve buys an equal amount of Treasury securities in that same market, it is not all that much different from the Treasury just printing up money. The only real difference is that our current monetary system allows the Federal Reserve Board to control how much money is in circulation. Whereas if the Treasury printed money and used that money directly in any way it wanted, there would be no independent control of our currency by the professional economists on the Federal Reserve Board. The politicians would be free to water down the value of our currency whenever they chose to do so—without outside interference. Dismantling the Federal Reserve System and allowing the Treasury to directly print money, instead of having to issue Treasury securities, could eliminate the debt, but at the expense of losing control of the money supply.

The debt exists as a mechanism in the form of Treasury securities to soak up cash from the open market to match the same amount as the Treasury is using to help fund additional federal programs. If the Federal Reserve, or some other government agency such as the Social Security Administration, does not step in to buy Treasury securities and, instead, those securities are purchased by the private sector, then money is being transferred from the private sector to the public sector to fund public programs. One difference between that and taxation is that the purchase of Treasury securities is voluntary. No one is forced to buy Treasury securities any more than they were forced to buy war bonds during World War II.

Since Treasury securities are short-term debt, they can either be sold at any time in the financial markets or held until maturity. Treasury securities have very low rates of return because they are considered to be highly secure inasmuch as they are directly backed by the federal government in the same sense that any registered bank's certificates of deposit are backed by the Federal Deposit Insurance Corporation (FDIC).

FINANCIAL MARKETS ALERT US TO EXCESSIVE FEDERAL DEBT

Our financial markets will warn us when federal debt starts to become excessive. To understand how this works, we must first consider how debt, such as public or private bonds, operates in money flow, and examine the inverse relationship between a bond's price and its interest rate. This is best understood by comparing new bonds with old bonds. Each old bond has a coupon amount that is paid at regular intervals, such as monthly, quarterly, or annually, regardless of that bond's current price on the bond market. The old bond's interest rate is applied to the bond's original price on the day it was issued, which in turn sets the fixed coupon value. For example, say that an old bond was originally sold for $2,000 with an annual interest rate of 4 percent so it pays a coupon of $80 annually. If the demand for bonds falls, their prices will fall. The fall in price does not affect the $80 coupon amount paid by the old bond. That $80 is still paid annually. An old $2,000 bond just issued at 4 percent would fall in value to $1,000 if new $2,000 bonds were suddenly offering 8 percent because some bad news caused a dramatic drop in demand for $2,000 bonds. In a relative sense you can think of it as the price of old bonds falling or the interest rate on new bonds rising. It is just two sides of the same coin. This simple example shows the inverse relationship between the price of the old bonds and the interest rate offered on the new bonds.

Saying that the government has issued too much debt implies that the supply of debt is becoming too great relative to the demand for debt. But if that were true, the price of government securities would be falling dramatically and the interest rate on government debt would be rising substantially. The open market for Treasury securities is not telling us that, but rather the opposite. The interest rates on Treasury securities remain quite low, even on the longer-term securities that are not directly affected by the Fed's open market operations. Our free enterprise system and open financial markets are still generating plenty of demand for government securities. The interest rates on longer-term government securities are at historic lows. The idea that the time is near when we will be overwhelmed by an excessive supply of government securities is not at all verified by the financial markets. The empirical evidence is saying exactly the opposite. That doesn't mean that we should be piling up mountains of more debt, but only that the size of our debt is not an immediate problem. Paying off public debt in the long run should be secondary to maintaining a healthy economy in the short run. Ultimately these two goals are compatible, insofar as maintaining a healthy economy in the short run will maximize tax revenues in the long run when everything else is accounted for.[107]

The key is in determining the optimal money flow. The elite can make America great (again) by investing in America through supporting higher tax rates for higher-income categories. Through their generous tax payments on the demand side and investments on the supply side, wealthy Americans can help maintain a healthy level of supply and demand. Poor money flow results in the well-known Keynesian liquidity

---

107   To express this idea, economists frequently use the phrase *ceteris paribus*, which in Latin means "everything else held constant."

trap discussed earlier,[108] where resources, especially labor resources, go unused, and equilibrium occurs only in a nonexistent, theoretical world of negative wages and negative interest rates.[109]

THE LIQUIDITY TRAP

Too often in economics we follow the misguided prescription of prolonging suffering to cleanse the body and make penitence. While it is sometimes reasonable to allow Joseph Schumpeter's creative destruction[110] to weed out weak businesses and elevate more productive and efficient businesses at the micro level on a day-to-day and year-to-year basis, there is no justification for, and nothing to be gained by, taking the entire economy into a prolonged recession at the macro level. Moreover, a locally owned restaurant may go out of business when the economy dips temporarily into a recession, even though that restaurant is efficient and sustainable in the long run. Amazon and Tesla have been able to operate in the red (deficit spending) for extended periods, because investors provided a large pool of cash, and not because they are necessarily more efficient or more in demand than the local mom-and-pop restaurant that was forced out of business in a brief recession.

The problem with waiting for the economy to return to an equilibrium on its own is that it may take a very long time, and it may stabilize at a level lower than full employment due to the liquidity trap. The liquidity

---

108   Krugman, Paul R. "It's Baaack: Japan's Slump and the Return of the Liquidity Trap." *Brookings Papers on Economic Activity*, No. 2 (1998): 137–205.

109   Real interest rates can be negative when nominal interest rates fall below the rate of inflation, but a negative nominal interest rate economy is not realistic.

110   For more on creative destruction, see http://www.investopedia.com/terms/c/creativedestruction.asp.

trap is where interest rates for risk-free assets have essentially reached zero and cannot fall any further. Since savers are generally not willing to pay a bank to hold their money, and the bank itself is not willing to lend out money at close to zero interest, the money piles up and is spent on neither consumption nor investment. Injecting more money into an economy in a liquidity trap is like stepping on the gas when your car is in neutral. The gears go around and around, but the car goes nowhere.

The problem is that as currently structured, the Federal Reserve System is designed to put money in the hands of investors, not consumers. If the economy is running at full capacity, investors will invest in new plant and equipment to try to satisfy the excess demand. But if the economy is in a recession, businesses will not be interested in adding another production line when their existing production lines are not being fully utilized. Moreover, consumers may be slow to respond to price adjustments. Even when prices fall significantly, it may take consumers several quarters to fully respond to a lower level of prices. Economic professors Gregory Mankiw of Harvard University and Ricardo Reis of the London School of Economics argue that it is information, and not the prices per se, that is sticky.[111]

One solution when faced with a liquidity trap with sticky prices and information is to use fiscal policy to direct the flow of money to consumers. As previously mentioned, consumers will then spend the money on cars, clothes, and restaurant meals. Unlike the rich, they will not just sit on the cash, or use it to buy expensive paintings and real estate, or trade existing stocks and bonds, all of which do not require additional production of goods and services.

---

111   Mankiw, N. Gregory, and Ricardo Reis. "Sticky Information versus Sticky Prices: A Proposal to Replace the New Keynesian Phillips Curve." *Quarterly Journal of Economics*, Vol. 117, No. 4 (2002): 1295–1328.

The production and productivity improvements forgone in a prolonged recession—lost by an unnecessary delay in returning to full employment—can never be made up. They will be permanently gone. The unnecessary delay just creates a permanent setback for the economy as a whole and for all of our individual businesses and families; it is pointless and unnecessary. At this point, economic policy must intervene.

Economic policy at the macro level must offset excesses at the micro level to get our economy back on an even keel. When our economy is operating at full capacity with strong demand and low unemployment, we need to fend off inflation by cutting back on unnecessary government expenditures and getting more money into the hands of businesses seeking to expand their plant and equipment to satisfy the excess demand for their products and services. In that circumstance, more money needs to flow to investment. Government should avoid crowding out private business. To increase productive capacity when demand is generally threatening to outstrip supply, investment incentives such as business tax cuts may be appropriate to encourage businesses to expand plant and equipment. If demand is getting too strong relative to supply, tax increases on individuals may help reduce inflationary pressure and restore a more appropriate level of money flow. Congress needs to preauthorize tax and spending adjustments so the economy can stay on an even keel regardless of which political party is in power. We must act to keep politics out of decisions that affect the health of our economy and allow the government to act quickly and decisively to counter economic downturns.

On the other hand, when demand for goods and services is weak and unused capacity is widespread, inventories rise, and businesses start cutting back production and laying off employees. The Federal Reserve buys Treasury securities through its New York offices to release more money into the economy and bring down short-term interest rates. However, businesses have no incentive to expand plant and equipment when they already have unused capacity, since they're not using all of the plant and equipment they already have. There is no incentive to add plant and equipment in such circumstances no matter how much "confidence" businesses might gain through additional tax incentives or nice-sounding pro-business government sound bites. Without a substantial increase in demand for goods and services, the Federal Reserve's expansionary monetary policy will be like pushing on a string. A better approach, as mentioned above and discussed below, is to use "My America" prosperity accounts to inject money directly into the economy to immediately increase the demand for goods and services.

In addition to monetary policy, fiscal policy must play its role in reviving the economy. Unemployment assistance programs should automatically adjust to the level and duration of unemployment. During severe long-lasting downturns, payments should be larger and for longer periods. The unemployed have high marginal propensities to consume, which means they tend to spend all the money they receive. Giving them money is highly effective in raising demand to get the economy back to full employment. Another way to get the economy back up to speed is through temporary government expenditures, such as for infrastructure spending on repairing roads, bridges, and tunnels. Where possible, these expenditures should involve public-private joint ventures to get the economy back up to speed. As long as the economy has substantial unused capacity, public expenditures complement, rather than crowd out, private expenditures. Once unemployment has fallen substantially and the economy is back up to full capacity, government should back off of unnecessary expenditures to avoid pushing the economy beyond what it is capable of producing. It must avoid generating inflation, as when too much money chases too few goods and services.

As mentioned earlier, economists call the rate of unemployment that is the lowest rate that can be achieved without triggering excessive inflation the non-accelerating inflation rate of unemployment (NAIRU). In the past, the NAIRU was assumed to be somewhere between 4.5 and 5 percent. However, the expanding global supply chain, more rapidly advancing technologies, and increasing automation have pushed the NAIRU significantly lower. It might now be possible to reach 4 percent unemployment or lower before wages and prices start rising rapidly.

This is particularly true because in the past energy shortages played an important role in generating inflation. The energy for our economy was primarily based on oil and natural gas, which were fixed in supply. But the combination of hydraulic fracturing (fracking) and rapidly falling prices for renewable energy has kept energy costs significantly lower for longer. Moreover, through the use of fracking, the United States is poised in the near future to produce more oil than any other country on earth. This, along with more economical renewable sources of energy, may enable us to sustain an unemployment rate as low as 4 percent and, at the same time, a moderate inflation rate of up to 4 percent without triggering runaway inflation.

HAVE FED CREATE INDIVIDUAL "MY AMERICA" ACCOUNTS

The Federal Reserve can stop excessive inflation quite effectively by raising interest rates. However, as mentioned earlier, when the economy is in a recession, the lowering of interest rates by having the Federal Reserve purchase Treasury securities in the New York financial markets is sometimes referred to as "pushing on a string," in not being very effective in quickly stimulating demand for goods and services. To provide the Federal Reserve with the ability to inject monetary stimulus more quickly and more directly into the far reaches of the economy, every person over the age of 18 with a Social Security number would be assigned a bank account directly with the Federal Reserve Bank. Such accounts could be called "My America" prosperity accounts to encourage their use. An initial $1,000 would be placed in each account, which would be treated as a minimum deposit that could not be withdrawn until after age 70. To help people become familiar with their account, all Internal Revenue Service (IRS) tax refunds would be deposited into these accounts. An individual could deposit additional money into their account up to a maximum annual limit, which could be adjusted from year to year depending upon the state of the economy.

To avoid disrupting commercial banking and to focus on the less affluent, the interest rate would only be applied to the first $10,000 of the account value. Funds above $10,000 would earn no interest. Most people have checking accounts with very little money in them, so the banks would not lose much in investible funds in phasing out paper checking accounts. At this point the $1,000 initial amount and the $10,000 upper limit are arbitrary. These numbers may be changed after more careful analysis and remain subject to change depending on economic conditions.

Each smartphone would be preregistered with the Federal Reserve through any post office. Transactions would be verified by both smartphone identification and a user-selected password, as well as fingerprint and/or iris recognition using the camera on the smartphone. In addition, there would be a 60-digit alphanumeric security code generated by an algorithm unique to the user and coordinated with the corresponding algorithm for that account at the Federal Reserve. After each transaction, the 60-digit security code would change both on the smartphone and in the corresponding Federal Reserve account so that no security code would be used more than once. A blockchain across all the account holder's communication devices (smartphone, laptop computer, desktop computer, etc.) could record each verified transaction in sync with their "My America" Federal Reserve Bank account.

Each year the IRS would deposit all tax refunds directly into these individual accounts.[112] Any money deposited by individuals into their accounts, any additional money injected into the accounts, and any interest earned could be withdrawn at any time. Only the initial $1,000 would have to be retained in the account until age 70.

This would allow for transactions between smartphones, similar to those used in Kenya's M-Pesa system of smartphone money transfers. The interest earned could be designated as tax-free. These Federal Reserve accounts could take the place of the old, often unprofitable, paper checking accounts that are holdovers from the 20th century. Eventually, these accounts could also replace cash, as smartphones replace wallets in people's pockets.

The Federal Reserve could then inject money directly into these accounts to provide stimulus as needed whenever a downturn developed, and recession threatened. These bank credits would be created by the monetary authority of the Federal Reserve out of "thin air"—with no taxation required. There would be no addition to the debt, because there would be no government securities issued. As long as the economy has unused capacity, the injection of cash would not trigger inflation. These cash payments could be referred to as *tax refund equivalence* payments, although everyone would get them, even those who paid no taxes. These accounts could be used to implement the late economist Milton Friedman's proposal of a negative income tax, which would especially help the poorest Americans. Such an approach would make the "My America" accounts very powerful in stimulating consumer demand using the least amount of money, because the poorest Americans have the highest marginal propensities to consume.

---

112   Such accounts could also be used to deliver a universal basic income (UBI) if a UBI law is passed by Congress and signed by the president.

Not surprisingly, Wall Street bankers prefer to have the stimulus money given to them, which they typically use to buy more stocks and bonds, which inflates stock and bond prices but does little to increase consumer demand for ordinary goods and services. During Japan's economic slump, Federal Reserve chair Ben Bernanke suggested that the Japanese government provide direct cash payments to Japanese citizens to stimulate demand. By implication he raised the idea of direct cash payments to consumers as an alternative to giving money created out of "thin air" to Wall Street bankers by buying Treasury securities during an economic downturn. Wall Street supporters responded to the idea of giving cash payments directly to consumers by coining the phrase "helicopter Ben," as if such a plan was equivalent to dropping money from helicopters. To belittle such "helicopter money" further, the bankers and their supporters posted "helicopter Ben" videos on YouTube.[113] But the critics of quantitative easing (known as QE) and other Federal Reserve injections of cash into the economy warned of a great inflation that never happened. The critics were wrong! Not only did QE help revive the American economy without significant inflation, but also a substantial proportion of the Fed's bond purchases was from European banks, so the Federal Reserve helped revive the Eurozone as well.

Direct cash payments through "My America" accounts would have a much quicker and bigger impact on consumer demand and require much less money than giving a lot of money to Wall Street bankers by having the Federal Reserve Bank buy Treasury securities in the New York financial markets. Consequently, it makes more sense to bypass the Wall Street bankers and give the money directly to the American people who

---

113   For example, see YouTube videos at https://www.youtube.com/watch?v=tqTLTHE-JEI8 and https://www.youtube.com/watch?v=UKU1RVwzqkA.

know best how to spend the money and, thereby, directly stimulate the economy by increasing the demand for goods and services.

Conversely, when inflation threatened, these individual "My America" bank accounts could offer attractive interest rates to absorb funds directly from the public to take money out of the economy and reduce excess demand. The high interest rates would cause people to put off consumption now for the prospect of greater consumption sometime in the future. At the same time, the Fed could pursue a mixed strategy to stimulate business investment by lowering the federal funds rate (discount rate) that banks pay for overnight loans, as well as the interest rate the Fed pays on the reserve funds that banks have at the Fed. Offering higher interest rates to consumers would reduce excess demand, while the lower rates on bank funds would make investment money available for expansion of plant and equipment, which would also help ease price pressure by increasing the supply of goods and services. Together the reduction in demand and increase in supply (over time) can ease pressure on prices and fend off inflation. The Fed can also engage in open market operations to buy or sell government securities. Econometric analysis can provide the Fed with guidance on getting exactly the right mix of these policy tools to achieve the Fed's objectives.

The Federal Reserve could be mandated to estimate the multiplier effect of each government program and proposed expenditure. It could then evaluate tax-expenditure combinations that could provide a balanced budget multiplier as needed to keep the economy on an even keel without increasing, and possibly even decreasing, the federal debt.

PROTECTING AND SECURING SOCIAL SECURITY

In addition to saving for a "rainy day," people must save for retirement. Many people rely primarily on our Social Security system to cover their

basic retirement expenses, and this growing trend is not helpful in ensuring a healthy overall economy. In the late 1970s and early 1980s, I worked
with one of my colleagues, Professor Meredith Scovill at the University
of Notre Dame, on a system dynamics model of the Social Security system.[114] Using nonlinear systems of differential equations and numeri-
cal integration, we simulated the fate of our Social Security system into
the future. Given the actual births that took place in the years up until
1975 and adjusting for death rates, we were able to simulate the number of people withdrawing money from the Social Security system into
the future. Our analysis suggested that the Social Security Trust Fund
would run out of money sometime after the baby boomer generation
reached retirement. The system was going to go into the red but would
come back into the black as the baby boomers died off.[115] We presented
our results at the Social Security Research Workshop in Williamsburg,
Virginia, in 1978.[116]

Research Director Fritz Scheuren, Wendy Alvey, and other Social
Security analysts took note of our results along with their own research
and that of other independent investigators. The Social Security
Administration maintained a systematic program of building up the
Social Security Trust Fund in anticipation of this revenue shortfall, and
Social Security was made immune from general budget deductions by

---

114   Marsh, Lawrence C., and Meredith Scovill. "Evaluating the Future of a Self-Financed
       Social Security System." *Modeling and Simulation*, Vol. 9. Proceedings of the 1978
       Pittsburgh Simulation Conference, Pittsburgh, Pennsylvania, 1978.

115   Although we did our analysis independently, the Social Security Administration
       research group paid for our travel and hotel accommodations.

116   Marsh, Lawrence C., and Meredith Scovill. "Using System Dynamics to Model the
       Social Security System." *NBER Workshop on Policy Analysis with Social Security
       Research Files*. Williamsburg, Virginia, March 15–17, 1978.

the Balanced Budget and Emergency Deficit Control Act of 1985, also known as the Gramm-Rudman-Hollings, or GRH, act.

The Social Security Administration has consistently and systematically collected more money through payroll and related sources than it has paid out in Social Security benefits. It has quietly purchased trillions of dollars in Treasury securities over the years to prepare for the baby boomers' retirements. However, baby boomer death rates have been lower than some expected, so the savings are not quite enough to cover benefits until the baby boomer generation is gone.

In 2017, the annual surplus was $44 billion. However, baby boomers have been retiring at a rapid rate with few workplace replacements, so the annual surplus dropped to $3 billion in 2018, and the OASDI trust fund reached a total of $2.895 trillion at the end of 2018.[117]

Falling fertility rates and lower immigration rates are reducing the earnings tax generated from tax revenues from the 6.2 percent Social Security tax rate on earnings. Meanwhile, the baby boomer bulge has begun entering the retirement years and is placing an ever-increasing demand for retirement benefits from the system. The Social Security Administration estimates that by 2034, Social Security benefits will need to be reduced to approximately 79 percent of their current values if nothing is done to augment the flow of money into the system. The system can either be sustained at lower benefit levels or adjusted to increase revenues.

One way to solve or help alleviate the temporary shortfall in Social Security revenues would be to remove or raise the $132,900 earnings cap that was set for 2019 and thereafter. Another would be to increase the tax rate on individuals from the 6.2 percent tax on earnings to 7.4

---

117   "Old-Age, Survivors, and Disability Insurance Trust Funds, 1957–2018." Social Security Administration. https://www.ssa.gov/oact/STATS/table4a3.html.

percent, with employers providing matching amounts.[118] An increase in the number of working-age immigrants entering the US labor force would also help increase the Social Security payroll tax revenues and help replace baby boomers in the workforce as they retire. Less-popular options would be to raise the retirement age from 65 to 70 or to significantly reduce Social Security benefits. The viability of Social Security is important not only to ensure adequate money flow to our senior citizens, but also to maintain sufficient demand for goods and services throughout our economy for a healthy and rapidly growing economy.

REPLACE INEFFICIENT PRIVATE-SECTOR HEALTH-CARE SYSTEM

Implementing the single-payer Medicare-for-all proposal could substantially reduce health-care costs. Senator Bernie Sanders's claim that Medicare administrative costs were only 2 percent while private insurance administrative costs have ranged from 12 to 18 percent has largely been verified by a PolitiFact investigation by Manuela Tobias.[119] Tobias reported that the 2017 annual Board of Trustees report for the Medicare Trust Funds showed Medicare expenditures of $678.7 billion for 2016 with $9.2 billion for "administrative costs." Tobias points out that this comes to a ratio of 1.4 percent (lower than the Sanders claim). She also noted from various official sources that private insurance administrative

---

118   The original Social Security 2100 Act proposal would apply a 7.4 percent earnings tax on all dollars up until $132,900 and after $400,000, but not the dollars in between. This would create a convenient doughnut hole to avoid annoying some politically important middle-class taxpayers.

119   Tobias, Manuela. "Comparing Administrative Costs for Private Insurance and Medicare." PolitiFact. www.politifact.com/truth-o-meter/statement/2017/sep/20/bernie-s/comparing-administrative-costs-private-insurance-a/.

costs ranged from a low of 11 percent in the large-group market to 20 percent in the individual market.

Price fixing, monopoly profits, advertising and promotion costs, and confusion over who is insuring whom for which benefits all drive up the cost of health care. Enrollment issues and determining what is covered, what is not, and how much the copay is can take up a lot of time and money that would not be consumed in a more straightforward system for health care.

Tobias also points out that Medicare uses the individual data already maintained by Social Security and a less aggressive approach to restricting payments. Nonetheless, along with the substantially lower health-care costs for equal or better treatment in other industrialized countries, these results indicate that a lot of money could be saved both by switching to a single-payer Medicare-for-all program and through negotiations with pharmaceutical companies to lower drug prices. Investing more in the National Institutes of Health, which funds a broad range of medical research in American universities, could help discover cures for a wider range of illnesses than those targeted by the pharmaceutical companies. Providing for the health-care needs of all Americans could reduce the incidence of illness, allowing them to lead more productive lives.

MAKE ESTATE TAXES MORE ATTRACTIVE

The new tax law that passed Congress in December 2017 doubled the exemption for the federal estate tax to $11.2 million starting with the 2018 tax year. The estate tax applies to less than two-tenths of 1 percent of deaths in the United States, and 99.8 percent of Americans pay no estate tax whatsoever. Even though the tax is supposed to help create a level playing field and equal opportunity for each new generation of Americans, it is reviled as the "death tax" by some of its detractors.

Perhaps a way to make the estate tax more palatable to the wealthy would be to allow them in advance of their death to direct their future estate tax payment to particular federal programs, with a checklist of such programs on IRS estate tax forms or on the IRS website. Those expecting to pay especially large sums could request that a bridge, road, school, or federal building be named after them. If the program required at least a $10 million tax payment and the wealthy person owed less in estate taxes than the required cutoff amount, then that person would be allowed the option of requiring the executor of their estate to pay an extra amount out of their estate to make them eligible for the program.

Wealthy individuals who want some sort of edifice to memorialize their lifework, but who don't want to raise their family's ire by failing to give all their wealth to their heirs, might secretly welcome such a tax program. Their heirs can't be mad at them if the IRS was going to take the money anyway. In fact, heirs might be proud that a nearby school is given the family name, especially if it was paid for with money that the heirs were not going to be able to get anyway. Such designations should be subject to the approval of the board or authority overseeing the school, federal building, et cetera. Note that money is fungible so the plan would not affect which projects were funded, but only the names given to those projects.

Instead of feeling like a sucker for paying such a substantial portion of federal tax revenues, a wealthy taxpayer might feel some pride in contributing to the nation. It could be called the Taxpayer Appreciation Program (TAP). In a sense it turns the estate tax into a win-win program where wealthy taxpayers and their families receive some recognition and appreciation for their contribution to the common good. Of course, the deceased taxpayer would have to either indicate their willingness to participate in the program in advance in their will or delegate that responsibility to the executor of their estate.

If states created similar programs for their inheritance taxes in recognizing those who make substantial tax payments, we may see a dramatic change in the attitude of those who pay the most in those taxes. As an heir to a massive inheritance, you could have the choice of having a government structure named either after the deceased or after yourself.[120]

But would such a plan be practical? Wouldn't it introduce a lot of complicated bureaucracy, red tape, and cost? In effect, the answer to these questions has already been provided by Kiva.org and in the fact that money is fungible. In his book *Development as Freedom*, Amartya Sen emphasizes the importance of access to credit.[121] Years ago, my wife and I loaned money to microfinance projects run by some poor women in a developing country through Kiva.org. When the money was paid back, we would then designate our loan money for another project.

But after a few years we got busy and didn't get around to designating someone to be the recipient of our loan money. It didn't matter. The funding process was separate from the labeling process. Funding was done first and labeling came after the fact.[122]

If Warren Buffett were to indicate his willingness to participate in the TAP program on the appropriate IRS form for designating a future estate tax payment in his name, then somewhere in the United States (hopefully near Omaha, Nebraska), an elementary school might

---

120   For a formula for establishing an optimal level of inheritance taxation, see Piketty, Thomas, and Emmanuel Saez. "A Theory of Optimal Inheritance Taxation." *Econometrica*, Vol. 81, No. 5 (September 2013): 1851–1886.

121   Sen, Amartya. *Development as Freedom*. New York: Anchor Books, 1999.

122   When questions were raised, Kiva made it clear that it allocates the money before donors select recipients. Since money is fungible, this ultimately makes no difference if all Kiva-approved projects are fully funded. This seems to be the case, because the projects offered at Kiva.org attract donors quickly and are generally fully funded in short order.

be designated the "Warren Buffett Elementary School." Alternatively, based on Buffett's ordered preferences and current project availability, authorities might dedicate the "Warren Buffett Bridge," the "Warren Buffett Tunnel," or the "Warren Buffett Federal Building." A section of some interstate highway could be designated the "Warren Buffett Expressway." Of course, you only get to die once, so you would only get one such edifice named in your honor under the TAP program. Kiva.org already has this labeling process highly computerized. The IRS could create similar software as a small addition to the computers in the IRS public relations office.[123]

THE LUMP OF LABOR FALLACY

A misguided approach to dealing with unemployment that is based on a static rather than a dynamic understanding of our economy is the *lump of labor fallacy*. According to this belief, an economy has only a set number of possible jobs for its population. Low-cost foreign labor and labor-substituting technologies can take jobs out of this static pool, leaving a long-term deficit in jobs for our current and future workers. Again, the static thinkers see the world as a fixed pie to be fought over in an I-win-you-lose struggle. Static thinkers complain that China is selling us products at prices that are too low. Would you go to the manager of your neighborhood grocery store and complain that the store's prices are too low? Would you tell the manager that you want to pay more so that the store can afford to hire more employees? But paying more for the same amount of groceries will not induce the grocery store to hire more workers. Static

---

123   For less wealthy individuals, we could follow the example of India, which each year emails taxpayers who have paid more than 100,000 rupees in taxes a formal "Certificate of Appreciation" for their patriotic contribution to the nation.

thinkers on both the left and the right suffer from this lump of labor fallacy. Too many Democrats and Republicans assume that there is a fixed number of jobs in this world and we need to fight over them. If money were made available to states for infrastructure improvements or some other fiscal stimulus when the economy needs it, we could maintain a proper money flow and keep most people employed. Full employment requires fiscal policy adjustments from time to time to keep the economy on track without triggering excessive inflation.

IMMIGRATION AND THE LAW OF COMPARATIVE ADVANTAGE

Dynamic thinkers see the world much differently than do the static thinkers. Immigrants and foreign businesses can be job creators along with national and local businesses in a win-win strategy. Economies can expand or contract. They can produce labor in the form of complements or substitutes. A higher proportion of immigrants start their own businesses than nonimmigrants. This is due partly to the self-selective nature of immigrants. Immigrants are not random draws from their home populations. Rather, on average, they tend to have more initiative and persistence, as well as greater imagination and creativity, than their fellow citizens.

Also, discrimination against immigrants can sometimes make it more difficult for an immigrant to obtain an established job, so immigrants are more likely to start their own businesses. It is not easy to leave behind your friends, relatives, and traditional culture and pursue success in a foreign country, which often requires learning a new language and adapting to a new culture; such a move takes determination. While poorly educated immigrants work at jobs in the hot sun picking fruits and vegetables or other such jobs that native workers shun, immigrants with better educations are more likely to be job creators. In either case, they contribute to the payroll tax in support of our Social Security and Medicare programs. Consequently, it is in the interests of Americans in retirement or nearing retirement to promote more immigration into our country. With more tax revenues coming from more workers, the tax rate on earnings could be reduced or at least not be increased. This would help all workers. Also, people are resources. When our economy has more resources to draw upon, we are all better off. More can be produced at lower prices. The price you pay for fruits and vegetables is inversely related to the availability of immigrant labor.

In this highly integrated, internet-driven world, David Ricardo's law of comparative advantage is as strong and powerful as ever.[124] Even if another country could produce every possible product and service at better quality and lower price than anyplace else, it cannot produce all things for all people, because human wants are unlimited. The most efficient countries produce what they are relatively most efficient at producing, while leaving the rest to other countries to produce. To express this concept on a very small scale, I may be a better house painter than my house painter and a better electrician than my electrician, but I don't have the time or energy to do all my own house painting and electrical work, not to mention all that yard work and plumbing repair.

The old economic idea that all people want is more money and wealth has been shown to be misguided. Once their basic needs are met, what they really want is a sense of purpose and recognition of their

---

124   Ricardo, David. *The Principles of Political Economy and Taxation.* J. M. Dent & Sons, 1911.

self-worth.[125] Even dogs, horses, and other animals show this tendency. Everyone wants to find something they are good at. No one wants to feel useless and unimportant. Some people like to do their own yard work. Some could easily pay others to do the job but get great satisfaction from mowing their own lawn and trimming their own bushes. Everyone finds their own niche. As the young folk used to say in the 1960s, "Different strokes for different folks." What makes me feel important may be of no interest to you. But that is why we can all find a way to fit into this world, thanks to the law of comparative advantage.

THE SHARED PRODUCTIVITY SPILLOVER EFFECT

William Baumol (1922–2017) explained that productivity is ultimately shared throughout the economy.[126] A violin player in a professional orchestra in Mozart's time was paid a salary representing very little real wealth. But someone playing that same tune on their violin in a professional orchestra today gets paid a lot more in real terms. Today's violin player has more wealth in terms of cars, electricity, and flush toilets than medieval kings and queens.

Baumol pointed out that productivity improvements are shared. Technological improvements in one industry will attract workers away from other industries, causing not only higher real wages in the new industry, but also higher real wages in the old industry. This works not

---

125   Listen to Mark Zuckerberg's 2017 commencement talk at Harvard University about self-worth at https://www.youtube.com/watch?v=QM-8l623AouM or read it here: http://news.harvard.edu/gazette/story/2017/05/mark-zuckerbergs-speech-as-written-for-harvards-class-of-2017/.

126   Baumol, William J. *The Cost Disease: Why Computers Get Cheaper and Health Care Doesn't.* New Haven, CT: Yale University Press, 2012.

only within a nation, but across nations as well. As explained previously, we know from the law of comparative advantage that even if everyone else is better at doing everything than you are, you can still find that niche that others have neither the time nor the interest in pursuing. Productivity improvements are important, not only for the individual, company, and industry in which those improvements occurred, but also for all other workers because of the spillover effect.

Don't underestimate the importance of this combination of comparative advantage and productivity spillover. What this implies is that structural unemployment is not the huge problem that it is made out to be. As the economy returns to full employment and demand continues to increase slowly, the effect will be not only to start to raise the wages of those already employed, but also to begin to open up opportunities for others who do not have much in the way of technical skills. The spillover effect of improved overall productivity can help even the uneducated get paid a decent wage to pick up gum wrappers, cigarette butts, and other trash around a nearby shopping center or some other such routine unskilled work.

Politicians sometimes argue that structural unemployment and skill-biased technical change make economic stimulus ineffective in alleviating unemployment during economic downturns. They argue that retraining must take place first before any stimulus would be able to bring about full employment. The problem with that argument is that it fails to recognize that the law of comparative advantage operates just as effectively between individuals as it does between countries.

Even if an individual or group of individuals is better at every possible productive activity than another individual or group of individuals, there are only twenty-four hours in the day, and no individual or group of individuals can satisfy all possible consumer demands if sufficiently stimulated. The fact that the United States in 2019 was experiencing the lowest unemployment rate in 18 years demonstrates this. The little residual unemployment that existed in 2019 was clearly frictional (transitioning between jobs).

However, it is still in our national interest to provide job training and enhanced educational opportunities for our citizens. An educated population is a common property resource that benefits everyone. A healthy, well-balanced economy can be a win-win for everyone, as the rising tide of economic activity raises all boats. It still makes sense to get a good education and improve your work-related skills, but the increased productivity that you engender by having increased your human capital will be shared with others to some degree down the line.

If you understand the lump of labor fallacy and the misguided nature of the I-win-you-lose strategy, you will realize that your hard work and success can indirectly help others as well through Baumol's spillover effect. Those who play I-win-you-lose resent free riders and hold back everyone, while those who are generous in pursuing the win-win strategy help others while helping themselves. By picking up the trash in your neighborhood, you protect your own property's value but also the property values of your neighbors. Ultimately, win-win wins and I-win-you-lose loses.

You not only benefit from investing in your own education, but the Baumol spillover effect ensures that you also benefit from the taxes you paid to help improve the education and productivity of others. Our economy inherently works to make sure that your generosity comes back to you. Improved productivity in our economy helps enhance the quality and variety of useful products, while competition drives prices lower and quality higher for everyone.

Investing in education is like a farmer's decision to invest in a future crop. Should a farmer spend a lot of money preparing her fields and then spend even more money for seed and fertilizer, or should she hold on to every penny and just hope that the crop will somehow seed and fertilize itself? Generating a bountiful harvest requires investing in the future by providing money flow. This is as true for the individual as it is for the nation as a whole.

FOURTH BRANCH OF GOVERNMENT FOR ECONOMIC POLICY

The major problem facing the economic system in this country is the political system. Politicians with vested interests and fanciful conceptions of economics—with little or no relationship to the real world—currently oversee the setting of economic policy. One admittedly fanciful solution would be to create a fourth branch of government in addition to the executive, legislative, and judicial branches. A constitutional amendment could convert the Federal Reserve System, the Congressional Budget Office, the General Accountability Office, and other similar government agencies concerned with our economic well-being into a new Prosperity Branch controlled by a board of professional economists.

In addition to monetary authority, they could be given a degree of control over fiscal policy, including the federal debt ceiling and the timing of preauthorized (e.g., infrastructure) spending and tax-rate adjustments (up or down for individuals or businesses). The new Prosperity Branch could be mandated to estimate the multiplier effect of each government program and proposed expenditure. It could then devise tax-expenditure combinations that would provide a balanced budget multiplier as needed to keep the economy on an even keel without increasing, and possibly even decreasing, the federal debt. It could be given veto power over federal budgets that were deemed harmful to the economy, given the state of the economy at any particular time.

The board members could serve for life or until voluntary resignation, such as in the Supreme Court. To avoid a banking industry takeover of the board and to ensure their professional qualifications, candidates for the board should be proposed by the board of the National Bureau of Economic Research (NBER), nominated by a vote of the NBER research associates, and approved by the US Senate. The Prosperity Branch could be tasked with an overall mandate to maximize our collective prosperity in our pursuit of life, liberty, and the pursuit of happiness as called for in our Declaration of Independence, in addition to the current mandate to minimize unemployment and avoid excessive inflation.

Of course, creating a fourth branch of government is highly unlikely.[127] But debating its merits could motivate us to at least strengthen the independence of the Federal Reserve.

SUMMARY, OVERVIEW, AND TRANSITION

This chapter discussed the role that fiscal and monetary policy play in determining and maintaining proper money flow in the economy. It emphasized the importance of the automatic stabilizers and the need to maintain them even when they result in higher federal debt during economic downturns. By the same token, deficit spending during economic expansions could lead to inflation if not properly managed. Whenever politically possible, a robust economy should be seen as an opportunity to pay off some of the debt burden.

continued

---

127   However, at one point in time women's suffrage was considered pie in the sky and gay marriage was just a pipe dream.

The permanent liquidity trap has hampered monetary policy in preventing interest rates from falling when the Federal Reserve attempts to inject more money into the economy through the New York financial markets. Establishing individual "My America" prosperity accounts could be a way to get around this problem and inject money directly into the hands of individual citizens whose spending can keep consumer demand strong enough to maintain a full-employment economy. Social Security, health care, education, and immigration are additional ways to reinforce the economy when demand is weak. Higher taxes combined with the TAP program are options to expand and maintain these programs.

Finally, a fourth branch of government could be seen as a solution to the failure of politicians to avoid partisan politics and keep the economy on an even keel—with full employment and a target level of inflation. The NBER could play a key role in the selection of the members of this board of governors.

The next chapter will examine how our economy interacts with the international economy in allocating resources efficiently through proper money flow between nations. Education, infrastructure, energy, and natural resources play key roles in the money flow between nations, as well as tariffs and foreign aid dollars. The idea that there is a fixed number of jobs in this world (that must be fought over) is—again—rejected.

The goal of maintaining "balanced trade" with each and every country is debunked, and the benefits of open and free trade are extolled. Our relationships with China and Mexico are particularly important in determining both our current and future international money flow. Barriers to trade are seen as obstacles to achieving efficient resource allocation where high-quality products are available at low prices.

CHAPTER 8

INTERNATIONAL MONEY FLOW: MONEY FLOWS BETWEEN NATIONS

P urchasing products from other countries usually requires purchasing their currency with US dollars to pay for the products in the local currency. Banks and online payment systems sometimes do this for their customers automatically. Money flows between nations just as it does between individuals, except with exchange rate adjustments as it crosses borders; in addition, tariffs and other trade restrictions can impede or encourage international money flow in terms of products, services, and investments.[128]

---

128 Haass, Richard. *A World in Disarray*. New York: Penguin Random House, 2017. Haass's book provides the essential backdrop of challenges to world order.

TRADE PROMOTES COMPETITION
IN FREE MARKETS

International trade is important for jobs, prices, and investment returns. In the past, politicians and the media have focused on how many jobs have been created and destroyed directly by international trade. This is an important but limited aspect of the impact of international trade on our economy. We focus on jobs because the impact is clear and immediate to a well-defined and easily identified group of people—namely, those who have lost or are likely to lose their jobs because of international trade.

The true number of jobs lost or created by trade is hard to actually determine, because so many products are jointly produced by the coming together of various components both directly and indirectly through international trade. There is no doubt that workers who lose their jobs due to international trade are likely to be hurt financially and to be very vocal and politically active in response to their circumstance. When their immediate financial difficulties are not adequately compensated by those who have achieved substantial benefits through exceptionally low prices and high investment returns from international trade, the losers have good cause to complain about government trade policies that have left them without a viable economic livelihood to feed, clothe, and shelter their families. This is especially true for blue-collar workers in rural areas with limited alternative job opportunities.

In the long run, winners need to share the benefits from international trade with the losers to avoid the political consequences of playing I-win-you-lose. As a nation we must be willing to allocate funds to provide retraining and relocation for workers who lose their jobs due to globalization and technological change.

Because only a portion of all potential voters actually vote, any large, strongly motivated group of losers can upset the applecart in any given election. To avoid economic setbacks and a debilitating political confrontation, winners must always be aware of the effect of economic policies on potential losers and make sure that everyone gets a reasonable share of the pie. This requires always keeping in mind the common good and not just personal financial benefits.[129]

Showing generosity, as well as respect and concern, for others are all key aspects of the win-win strategy. The slow-moving world of the past has now been replaced with a much more rapidly changing economy where keeping everyone on board is essential for smooth economic progress in a pro-growth strategy. More often than not, greed slows down economic progress while generosity greases its wheels. In the long run, only the win-win strategy works.

Politicians and political pundits continue to make the lump of labor fallacy in insisting that there is somehow a fixed number of jobs, when empirical evidence continues to demonstrate that this is not the case. Politicians blame unfair trade practices rather than face their own responsibility to provide adequate fiscal stimulus when the economy goes into an occasional slump. Trade allows for increased economic efficiency through the division and specialization of production, which lowers prices. A trade imbalance should not be used as an excuse for inadequate fiscal stimulus when an economy is not at full employment.

EDUCATION AND INFRASTRUCTURE INVESTMENT

Countries have both a practical and a patriotic duty to invest in their youth and in their infrastructure. President Eisenhower understood this in the early 1950s when he signed the National Defense Education Act

---

129   Reich, Robert B. *The Common Good*. New York: Penguin Random House, 2018.

that provided funds for GIs leaving military service after World War II to obtain additional education at various colleges, schools, and institutes. This was complemented by the establishment of the Eisenhower System of Interstate and Defense Highways, which was a direct result of General Eisenhower's astonishment toward the end of World War II at the efficient German autobahn system that allowed German troops and materials to move quickly between east and west across Germany.

When a recession threatens, money flow in the form of education and infrastructure investment is essential for heading off a recession with potentially high levels of unemployment. At the end of World War II, many economists believed that our returning GIs would face massive unemployment as our economy returned to prewar levels. Instead, under President Eisenhower's leadership, the 1950s proved to be a period of full employment and widely shared rapid economic growth. Today, investing in education and infrastructure can be a good investment for America, especially after such a long period of political gridlock and "starve the beast" politics.

Other countries in Europe and Asia are investing heavily in their infrastructure. They know that to be competitive, one has to actually compete and not fall behind in basic infrastructure. China has been especially proactive in investing in its future with modern, up-to-date ports, airports, roads, bridges, tunnels, and rail lines for high-speed trains.

In real terms, the biggest burden being left for future generations in the United States is not the public debt, but our own crumbling and out-of-date roads, bridges, railroads, ports, and airports. An economy running at top speed on all cylinders is able to pay down its debt, while a poorly performing economy with high unemployment and lots of unused capacity will only see its debt rise as tax revenues fall. Also, it is important to focus on the ratio of debt to GDP, rather than on the amount of debt per se. Even if the amount of debt holds constant or even rises slowly, if GDP is rising faster, then the debt will eventually become a much smaller proportion of GDP.

GENEROSITY AND SHARED PROSPERITY

The principle of shared prosperity applies not only within nations, but also between nations. After World War I, the Allies demanded reparations from Germany amounting to 269 billion gold marks, or the equivalent of $393.6 billion in 2005 US dollars.[130] This was a classic case of pursuing the I-win-you-lose strategy. The German economy suffered along with the German people, and ultimately the result was World War II. After World War II, in spite of the widespread destruction and massacre of millions of innocent lives, the Allies set aside bitterness and potential retribution and, instead, generously provided support such as the Marshall Plan to the defeated Germans. The money flow not only enabled the German economy to recover, but also provided a source of demand for American products, especially in the late 1940s and 1950s. Compensating the loser takes away their ability to play the victim. When we work together to help one another and support one another, there are no losers. We all win. Economic progress requires that adequate money flow must go to everyone, not just within a nation but also between nations and across all international boundaries.[131]

A similar approach was used in the restoration of Japan, showing once again the importance of the win-win strategy both within and across international boundaries. Right after World War II, America initially

---

130   See https://simple.wikipedia.org/wiki/World_War_I_reparations.

131   Slaughter, Anne-Marie. *The Chessboard and the Web*. New Haven, CT: Yale University Press, 2017. Slaughter's book explains the growing power of networks and information technology that cuts across borders in the increasing connectedness of the world.

imported some shoddily made products from Japan. The ungenerous response was Americans' use of the phrase "Made in Japan" to mean any poorly made product, no matter what its source. However, in response to this national insult, instead of sending terrorists and suicide bombers to America, the Japanese responded by sending high-quality Toyotas and Hondas. The derogatory "Made in Japan" phrase was quickly dropped. Similarly, the Polish people responded to "Polish jokes" that were (unfortunately) once popular in America by producing one of the best education systems in the world.[132]

We even had to deal with poor-quality products here at home. When American car companies switched from making tanks and military trucks for the war to making cars and light trucks for consumers, they produced some elegant-looking, but relatively unreliable, vehicles. I loved my 1958 Chevy, which was almost as cool as the more popular 1957 Chevy but without the elaborate tail fins. However, the gas mileage was terrible, the car developed mechanical problems, and it rusted easily. Without Japanese or other foreign competition, it might have been a long time before America came up with better-quality cars at more reasonable prices.[133]

Another good example of the effectiveness and beneficence of the win-win strategy was demonstrated in the United States assisting Mexico in the mid-1990s. In 1994, the Mexican government followed its usual election-year strategy of going into debt to bolster the financial

---

132   Finland, Poland, and South Korea pursued significantly different educational strategies to achieve high scores in the Programme for International Student Assessment (PISA) rankings.

133   Some of this was due to American quality control expert Edwards Deming, who ended up helping the Japanese after his systematic methods of achieving and maintaining high-quality control standards were disingenuously demurred, rejected, and/ or ignored by American car companies.

circumstances of its people through a series of programs to help the poor and middle class. Under normal circumstances, the debt level was manageable; but a series of political problems undermined the government and the stability of the Mexican peso. In particular, the Zapatista Army of National Liberation declared war on the government.

In March 1994, the PRI presidential candidate Luis Donaldo Colosio was assassinated in Tijuana. The combination of the financial extravagance and political instability undermined the value of the peso. Foreign investors began withdrawing funds from Mexico. Ultimately the Mexican government was forced to devalue its currency on December 20, 1994. Instead of calming the financial markets, investors not only continued to withdraw funds at a rapid pace but also started removing their money from emerging markets, especially Latin American markets, generally.

The Clinton administration viewed this situation with alarm. Economic advisors Robert Rubin, Alan Greenspan, and Lawrence Summers called for a $50 billion bailout of Mexico to prevent the spread of the "peso crisis" and avoid a massive flow of immigrants illegally crossing over the US southern border.[134] In January 1995, the United States organized a $50 billion financial package of loan guarantees for Mexico's public debt with the cooperation of the G7 countries and the Bank for International Settlements. The loan-guarantee package was overseen by the International Monetary Fund. Although the Mexican economy had a severe recession, the crisis was contained. The loans were repaid in full and earned a profit of $600 million. As in the case of Germany and Japan after World War II, the United States acted generously to stabilize

---

134   For additional details, see https://en.wikipedia.org/wiki/Mexican_peso_crisis.

a collapsing economy. Mexico benefited, but so did the United States. It was clearly another win-win situation.[135]

THE JOBS-VERSUS-PRICES TRADE-OFF

While jobs are very important, so too are prices. If you look carefully around your house, you are likely to find many articles of clothing and other objects with the words "Made in China" or "Made in Mexico," or words indicating that they were made in some other foreign country. The implication of so many foreign-made items in your home is that they were available at Walmart, Costco, Sam's Club, Sears, Kohl's, K-Mart, Amazon, eBay, and many, many other such retail establishments, because they were less expensive and of sufficient quality to make it worth your while to purchase them. Foreign countries selling their products in America not only provide quality products at low prices, but also force American companies to compete in terms of price and quality.

When working properly, the free enterprise system ultimately helps make everyone better off no matter where in the world they happen to be. A fundamental principle of John Rawls's *Theory of Justice* is to help the least advantaged.[136] Both Steve Bannon's "America First" policy and the "buy local" movement sometimes violate this principle with their "us versus them" perspective.[137]

---

135   For an excellent insightful review of this and the other financial crises around the world, see: Geithner, Timothy F. *Stress Test: Reflections on Financial Crises*. New York: Crown Publishers, 2014.

136   Rawls, John. *A Theory of Justice*. Cambridge, MA: Belknap Press, 1971.

137   Bremmer, Ian. *Us versus Them: The Failure of Globalism*. New York: Penguin Random House, 2018.

For a while, many least-advantaged people lived in China. They got work at low wages, but as their economy improved, their wages rose, and the low-wage work was transferred to Vietnam and other disadvantaged venues. Ironically, birth rates tend to fall rather dramatically as a country's economy improves and its citizens are made better off. This automatic reduction in the supply of workers drives wages up. Eventually, with free-trade and full-employment policies, there will no longer be any low-wage workers in the world. But maintaining full employment everywhere and an overall average wage growth of approximately 4 percent annually requires adequate money flow both within and between nations.

Professor William Baumol shows that pay increases from increased productivity in industry are passed along to "violin players" and others who had nothing to do with that increase in productivity. But the same is true on the consumption side as well. Businesses and their employees work hard to provide high-quality products at low prices, but under our free enterprise system, it is the consumer who ultimately benefits—and at the end of the day we are all consumers. Although we like to think of free enterprise as rewarding individuals for hard work and creativity, the reality is that the free enterprise system joins us together in a way that makes us all free riders in both production and consumption. Just as the violin player's salary rose as the productivity of other workers increased, and just as the price and quality of goods and services improved without the violin player's help, the violin player benefited as a free rider in our free enterprise system. In the future, as robots and artificial intelligence algorithms take over both physical and mental work, we should keep in mind that the free enterprise system does not reject free riders but embraces them.[138] We think that we are working hard to benefit ourselves by making productivity improvements and beating our competitors by offering better-quality products at lower prices, but we are really benefiting everyone. This is true both within a nation and across nations.[139]

MONEY FLOW STIMULATES CONSUMPTION AND INVESTMENT

From 2000 until 2014, China actively supported its currency in international money markets to keep the yuan (aka renminbi) from rising in value so that Chinese products would remain relatively inexpensive in international markets. This policy enabled millions of Chinese workers to obtain jobs and prosper in China's growing economy. China currency manipulation involved using US dollars (earned by selling Chinese products to Americans) to purchase US Treasury securities, which then sent those dollars back into the American economy. If these dollars had been made available through government spending, they would have put Americans to work in other jobs in other industries. China tossed us the ball, but we failed to run with it. Rather than putting that money to use, Congress failed to allocate that money to fund infrastructure repairs and other badly needed job-creating programs here in the United States.

---

138   Picking up trash in the street in your neighborhood helps protect your property's value, but also the property values of your neighbors. Following the win-win strategy, you are also glad to be protecting the property values of your neighbors. On the other hand, following the "I-win-you-lose" strategy means that you ignore the trash, because you don't want those "free-riding" neighbors to benefit from your efforts. When it comes to protecting property values, "win-win" wins and "I-win-you-lose" loses.

139   In other words, we will all be better off if the Chinese cure cancer or devise a battery with much better electrical storage capability, and so on.

China has also invested in other countries, particularly in other parts of Asia and Africa, but also in Australia, Canada, and Russia.[140]

However, between the end of 2016, when a US dollar could buy about 7 yuan, until mid-April of 2018, when a dollar was worth only 6.30 yuan, China has allowed the yuan to rise in value relative to the US dollar and other foreign currencies in international markets, until it responded to President Trump's decision to start a trade war with China in March 2018. Since then the number of yuan per dollar has risen abruptly back above 7 yuan per dollar. China has recognized the need to switch from an economy primarily based on exporting to other countries to an economy with a strong domestic consumer base. This switch in policy is a natural one for a developing economy, but also good politically both to reduce China's dependence on demand from other countries and to reward its growing middle class with increased goods and services. This has helped the Chinese leadership to deflect criticism and maintain control over its citizens. The long-term goal of a democratic China may have to take second place to the need to maintain a stable and peaceful China.

In any case, in future years we will see more demand for goods and services, including selling more US exports to China. Going forward, we should be able to see a more balanced money flow between China and the United States. However, tariff wars upset the prospects for increased exports to China and generally introduce more uncertainty and instability into the market for agricultural and other American products.

By resolving the trade war with China, we can refocus our efforts to gain greater market access, improved intellectual property rights protection, and more investment opportunities in China. The intellectual

---

140   For a list of China foreign direct investments from 2004 to 2010, see http://www.cnbc.com/2012/05/23/Top-10-Countries-for-Chinese-Investments.html.

property rights issue is a particularly interesting one, in that over the years US patents—which were supposed to promote innovation by allowing investors time to recoup investments—have become extended to the point that they suppress rather than encourage innovation. China's concerns in this regard should be taken seriously, and both countries should engage in a reasonable debate about this issue and find a mutually acceptable agreement.

Mexico is another policy concern that is a day late and a dollar short, so to speak. Prior to 2008, before the economic downturn in the United States, there was a net inflow of immigrants from Mexico coming into the United States. While the unemployment rate in the United States stayed below 4 percent throughout 2018 and much of 2019, at the same time Mexico also had an unemployment rate well below 4 percent. Consequently, since 2008 the number of Mexican nationals *leaving* the United States has exceeded the number entering, thus resulting in a net outflow. These days, most immigrants seeking to cross the southern border of the United States are from El Salvador, Honduras, Guatemala, and Nicaragua.

In 2016, China, Mexico, and Canada each accounted for roughly 15 percent of total US imports and exports, or a combined 45 percent. Mexico imported about $212 billion in US products, while Canada imported $245 billion, and China $104 billion. Of the inputs used to produce Mexican finished goods, about 40 percent of them come from the United States. Trade with Canada generates 24 percent of US exports and supports 8.27 million jobs in the United States—or about 4.54 percent of all US jobs.[141] A trade-stifling tariff war with any or all

---

141   See the 2014 study by Peter B. Dixon and Maureen T. Rimmer of the Centre of Policy Studies at Victoria University: https://www.copsmodels.com/pdf/canada_trade_2013.pdf.

of these key trading partners would result in substantial job losses in the United States.

As long as needs are unlimited and potential customers exist somewhere, a dynamic economic strategy can increase demand for goods and services. A politically unrealistic (to say the least) thought experiment would be to consider carpet-bombing developing countries with dollar bills to generate demand for our goods and services. The increase in supply of dollars abroad would reduce the price of the dollar on international markets, which would make our products cheaper to purchase with foreign currencies. As long as that demand does not outstrip our productive capacity to satisfy it, that infusion of dollars would generate more American jobs—it would not result in inflation. Of course, I am not recommending this. It is just a thought experiment.

In effect, this is exactly what our foreign aid assistance is designed to do. In fact, some American aid requires that the money be spent directly on the purchase of American products, which directly translates into an increase in American jobs. Our 2017 foreign aid budget breaks down into $25.6 billion for economic development assistance and $16.8 billion for security, which totals to about 1 percent of our overall budget of $4.15 trillion.[142] In other words, our foreign aid program is a win-win strategy. I bomb your village with dollar bills, and you bomb my village with demand for products, which produces jobs. Who is losing here? No one. In practice, foreign aid is not dropped from airplanes but is designated for specific projects and often requires the purchase of US products. Of course, from an economic efficiency point of view, it would be better to allow the recipients of the financial assistance to decide how to spend it.

---

142   For a detailed breakdown, see https://www.washingtonpost.com/graphics/world/which-countries-get-the-most-foreign-aid/.

Of course, one can always overdo a good thing. Carpet-bombing too many countries with dollar bills too often could create excess world demand generally and produce runaway inflation. The more money flows abroad, the less valuable our currency becomes. The dollar will drop in value in response to the increase in the supply of dollars. We must keep in mind that making our goods cheaper for foreigners to purchase also makes foreign goods more expensive for us to purchase. If there is one fundamental principle we must learn, it is this: our money flow policies require a balance that must always be constantly adjusted and updated to reflect the current state of the economy, both nationally and internationally. To a great extent, it is often best to let the free enterprise system adjust our currency's value in foreign exchange markets, with little or no interference or manipulation.

What about creating a common currency? The European experience has clearly demonstrated that having different nations share the same currency makes trade between nations easier, but makes achieving the optimal money flow *within* each nation a lot more difficult.[143] It is not sufficient for money, goods, and services to flow across borders. Labor must also be willing and able to move freely. People like to assume that, everything else being equal, everyone else would want to live in their country. In reality, most people have cultural, personal, and family ties that keep them strongly attached to their own home country. In the long run, a common currency only works with a sufficiently mobile labor force where workers move easily across borders. The euro will continue

---

143   Krugman, Paul. *End This Depression Now!* New York: W. W. Norton & Company, 2012. Krugman's book explains the problem with a common currency for different nations.

to create economic distortions and disruptions until Europeans become a lot more multilingual, multicultural, and mobile.[144]

One factor that depresses labor mobility is the excessive use of non-compete clauses in labor contracts. The original justification of such clauses was to protect trade secrets and encourage job training, but such clauses are now used widely to discourage competition and labor mobility. Any pro-growth policy should include passing laws to severely limit the use of noncompete clauses in contracts.

A key factor in productivity and economic growth is population growth. Without a growing population, an economy is unable to provide the young and dynamic workforce needed to rapidly incorporate new technologies and support its elderly population. Japan, Germany, Italy, Spain, most Eastern European countries, and Russia are all losing population as their citizens become older and gradually die off. The United States would be losing population if it were not for immigration. Japan is using robotics to substitute more aggressively for population decline with very little immigration.

On the other hand, Germany has been much more open to immigrants and hopes to incorporate them smoothly into its labor markets to generate the tax revenues needed to support its aging population of retirees. Italy and Spain are facing low birth rates but have recently experienced a substantial increase in immigration. Russia is suffering from a combination of low birth rates, high abortion rates, relatively high death

---

144   For example, Ireland had 4,000 Polish-born people in 2002 and 120,000 by 2010. While some managed to assimilate rather well, other Polish migrant workers have faced a significant amount of cultural discrimination in Ireland. See http://www.irishtimes.com/news/social-affairs/migrant-workers-in-ireland-face-systemic-exploitation-1.2444681.

rates, little immigration, and some degree of emigration—especially among its young people, who seek greater opportunities abroad.

In the United States, we've become accustomed to rising per capita income and gross domestic product (GDP). But population growth and productivity increases are the most important factors in driving such improvements in human well-being, and things are looking tenuous. Over the last decade, productivity in the United States has hardly grown at all. A country with stagnant productivity, a declining population, and an aging population with falling rates of labor market participation cannot expect to see its per capita GDP rise. If anything, it could well fall in the coming years, especially if immigration stalls or declines.

Without more workers paying the earnings tax, Social Security and Medicare may have to be substantially cut back until the baby boomers die off. Just because you reliably paid into the system for years and years does not guarantee that the system will be able to generate the revenues needed to help pay for your retirement or health care, unless more workers come from somewhere or productivity increases dramatically. Clearly from a purely economic point of view, it is in our national interest to *promote* immigration, not discourage it.

ENERGY AND NATURAL RESOURCES

The Russian economy continues to be heavily dependent on mining natural resources, with limited expansion into other areas. A large portion of the Russian government's revenue comes from fossil fuels, especially oil and natural gas. The drop in fossil fuel prices in recent decades has significantly hurt the Russian budget. To distract from the poor conditions faced by the Russian middle class and the aging population, Russia has pursued a policy of focusing the country's attention on international affairs in a traditional strategy of asking its people to sacrifice internal freedom in order to protect its external freedom, national sovereignty, and national dignity. When Russia felt threatened by Ukraine's attempt to integrate more closely with the European Union, Russia promoted a rebellion in western Ukraine and in 2014 took Crimea from Ukraine. This provided a convenient distraction from the Russian government's efforts to gain control over television and radio, as well as to restrict opposing candidates in Russian elections. False news reports and unfounded criminal charges have been used to promote anger and vilification of opponents. In like manner, authoritarian leaders from Nicolás Maduro in Venezuela to Kim Jong Un in North Korea have used similar strategies to maintain their power, citing the United States as a dangerous enemy plotting to take control of their country.

Since the United States is the greatest consumer of oil in the world, demand for oil within the United States has a major impact on world oil prices. Anything that can be done to reduce the demand for oil in the United States will cause world oil prices to drop. At the same time, hydraulic fracturing (fracking) has increased American production of crude oil to levels rivaled only by Saudi Arabia and Russia. Traditionally, the international price of oil (Brent) is several dollars higher per barrel than West Texas Intermediate, which is known in financial markets as WTI. Brent and WTI are frequently compared in financial reports and at stock exchanges.

Higher US gasoline taxes could lower the Brent price by lowering US demand for crude oil in international markets and raising the US price for gasoline at the pump. This would suppress the revenues of Russia, Venezuela, and other oil-exporting countries while raising US revenues. It would also encourage environmentally friendly alternative sources of energy—such as solar and wind—as well as advances in battery technology and our electric vehicle industry, and thus provide more job opportunities.

China took the advice that Al Gore[145] and Tom Friedman[146] gave to the United States to lead the world in the development of renewable energy technologies—especially in the development and manufacturing of electric vehicles. Unfortunately, the US government largely ignored such advice. Many politicians were stuck in the old fossil fuel mind-set, where they themselves made a great deal of money and had personal vested interests. President Trump tried to revive the coal industry and placed tariffs on imports of solar panels from China instead of providing support for basic research and incentives for the development of the renewable energy industry. It seems, as a country, we have been more interested in trying to hang on to the past than to move forward into the 21st century. The downside? We can only watch from the sidelines as China develops new technologies that the US government lacked the imagination to envision.

EFFICIENT ECONOMIC DEVELOPMENT

Too often economists view economic development as the problem of organizing an economy to maximize a country's GDP. But GDP does not measure the quantity of goods and services that our citizens are consuming; it measures what they produce. If the goal is to maximize production for someone else, then GDP serves as a useful measure. But if we are concerned with the welfare of our people, then gross national product (GNP) is a more appropriate measure of what our people are actually consuming. Before 1990 we focused on GNP, but large multinational corporations and Wall Street bankers, who have dominated our

---

145   Gore, Al. *An Inconvenient Truth.* Emmaus, PA: Rodale, 2006.

146   Friedman, Thomas L. *Hot, Flat, and Crowded.* New York: Picador, 2009.

economic and political discourse, preferred to focus on the GDP measure, because it more accurately measures what we are producing.

Moreover, this top-down view ignores the source of wealth creation. Nature takes an entirely different approach. The classic example is the ant colony. The queen ant does not hand down orders from above. Instead, ants react to stimuli in their immediate surroundings to instinctively organize themselves with great efficiency at the local level. Successful economies operate in much the same way. Encouraging local businesses to flourish is essential for maximizing the creativity and productivity of each person. Even in the largest, most developed economies, most workers are employed by small businesses or are self-employed. Only a small portion work for large enterprises.

China has been moving quickly to establish itself as a key economic player in the 21st century. The economies of China and the United States are already becoming highly integrated. American officials complain that China is manipulating its currency to sell its products to American consumers at excessively low prices. Many of the cheap products that China produces are no longer made in America. In a sense, all this is reminiscent of what happened in Japan right after World War II. Japanese companies exported a torrent of cheap products to the United States. As mentioned earlier, the term "Made in Japan" was used to refer to any cheap and useless product. The Japanese were insulted, so they switched gears and, with the advice of American quality control expert Edwards Deming, they created a host of high-quality automotive and electronic products. Now history is repeating itself with China. Cheap product production is moving over to Vietnam, Cambodia, Bangladesh, and other low-wage countries as China moves ahead to produce higher-quality products.

The other highly contentious issue with China is democracy. You may recall the difference between external freedom (freedom from foreign domination) and internal freedom (democracy). Throughout history, people have sacrificed internal freedom in order to secure their external freedom—the previous example being Russia and other authoritarian countries. With China's history of being exploited by foreign powers, as well as having to combat its own internal turmoil, we should not be surprised by its reluctance to loosen up its central controls. As with Iran, the best policy may be for democratic countries to privately encourage Chinese leaders to incorporate more democracy, yet to avoid interfering with China's internal affairs.[147]

An earlier discussion of microfinance through Kiva.org[148] was designed to point out how the internet frees each citizen to establish their own "foreign policy" by directly loaning money to individuals wishing to start or expand businesses in developing countries—and even in low-income areas in the United States. One way to reduce the number of mischief makers around the world is to keep everyone busy with business. Surely, getting rich is more fun than blowing yourself up in a suicide bombing. In the next section, we will consider how US foreign aid policy has been helpful and hurtful in this regard.

HAVE 50 YEARS OF US AID MONEY STYMIED AFRICAN GROWTH?

Unfortunately, too much of the foreign aid money flowing to Africa has been controlled by corrupt government officials who demand bribes and payoffs. This top-down organization and control generally discourages and often blocks business development at the bottom. Friends, clans, and tribes of top officials benefit on the basis of their connections to those in

---

147   Polk, William R. *Understanding Iran*. New York: Palgrave-Macmillan, 2009.

148   Anderson, Kaila. "Free Market Meets Altruism in Kiva." *The Orange County Register*. March 12, 2010.

power, instead of their competitive efficiency and productivity. In countries where government officials control foreign aid and natural resource wealth, the focus becomes how to divide up the economic pie rather than how to enlarge it. Journalist Oliver Bullough provides an eye-opening account of how money laundering has facilitated graft and corruption by people with power and influence primarily in African and Middle Eastern countries in his book *Moneyland*.[149]

And the problems are not only internal. In her book *Dead Aid*,[150] economist Dambisa Moyo argues that foreign aid to Africa has not just been ineffective, but has also actually blocked African economic development. Are we not only throwing US taxpayer money down the drain but also hurting Africans in the process? In recent years, economists have become increasingly aware that natural resources, especially oil resources, can be a curse on a country rather than a blessing. Here's why. Foreign money (the United States purchasing oil, for example) must first be exchanged for local currency before it can buy local goods (oil). Such large purchases of the local currency can drive up its price in the international foreign exchange markets. Thus, foreign money seeking to purchase a nation's oil can drive up the value of the local currency to the point that its products become too expensive to sell in international markets. Moyo points out that this problem, which is known to economists as the *Dutch disease*,[151] can also be caused by money pouring into an economy through foreign aid.

The Economist came up with the term "Dutch disease" to describe the deterioration of the manufacturing sector in the Netherlands after

---

149   Bullough, Oliver. *Moneyland*. London: Profile Books, Ltd., 2018.

150   Moyo, Dambisa. *Dead Aid*. New York: Farrar, Straus & Giroux, 2009.

151   "The Dutch Disease." *The Economist*. November 26, 1977.

a large natural gas field was developed there with the help of foreign oil companies. Examples of countries affected by the Dutch disease outside of Africa include Venezuela and Iran. Some African countries with oil, gold, or diamonds have been subject to a double whammy of the natural resource curse and foreign aid dependency.

Foreign aid not only drives up the value of the local currency to block the country's export growth, but is also frequently tied to the required purchase of donor country commodities, such as US grain, to further drive a nail in the coffin of the country's economy by displacing local grain farmers. Moyo notes another example as she cites the well-intentioned donation of $1 million worth of (imported) mosquito netting that provided immediate medical benefits—but also destroyed a nascent mosquito net industry that employed many Africans. Moreover, destroying the netting industry eliminated the source of replacement netting, which will be needed when the donated netting eventually wears out and falls apart. Finally, a well-known example is that of Toms Shoes, which offered to donate a pair of shoes for each pair purchased and ended up destroying local shoe industries by dumping aid-type (imported) shoes in African countries.

In a poor democratic country without natural resources or foreign aid, people who are determined to become rich do not go into government. When a democratic government has no money except the little it can collect from its poor citizens, politicians make a personal sacrifice by going into politics, where they generally make a lot less money than in the private sector. Moreover, the citizens demand that the money be spent to their benefit and not squandered. (With no natural resources or foreign aid, the primary way to increase a country's wealth is to build the country's human capital by educating its people.)

Conversely, when the money arrives top-down—from foreign sources—instead of emerging from the bottom up, corrupt politicians have first crack at the money and can dispose of the rest as patronage for their supporters. Controlling the money means controlling the voters, instead of the other way around. We have recently seen this problem develop in other countries. In Afghanistan, foreign aid money has been misdirected by corrupt officials. Corruption in Haiti blocked distribution of much-needed emergency medical supplies from the Port-au-Prince airport following an earthquake—until the media got wind of the story.[152]

Moyo reviews other explanations for the poor economic performance of many African countries and essentially shows them to be symptoms rather than the cause of the problem. She argues that foreign aid fosters dependency similar to welfare dependency. Until African countries have to stand on their own two feet, they will never attain economic maturity. Moyo's recommendations include gradually weaning Africa off of foreign aid and removing obstacles such as agricultural subsidies in donor countries that unfairly undermine African economic development.

CAN FREE MARKETS AND LOCAL BUSINESSES CONVERT POVERTY INTO PROSPERITY WHEN FOREIGN AID FAILS?

The World Bank's annual report, *Doing Business*, ranks countries on the basis of how easy it is to start and run a business in each country. In their book *The Aid Trap*,[153] Professors Glenn Hubbard and William Duggan point out that countries that rank high in *Doing Business* have

---

152   Associated Press. "Tons of Food Aid Rotting in Haiti Ports." *Barbados Free Press.* March 7, 2008.

153   Hubbard, Glenn, and William Duggan. *The Aid Trap.* New York: Columbia University Press, 2009.

more prosperity and much less poverty than countries that rank low.[154] They review the unlikely emergence of prosperity in modern times after millennia of humans struggled for survival where poverty was a welcomed alternative to the only other common outcome—early death. The business system was suppressed throughout history by other competing systems, such as the tribal, despotic, feudal, national socialist, and pure socialist systems. At first the business system developed only in isolated pockets where the antibusiness forces were weak, such as in Venice in Southern Europe and Amsterdam in Northern Europe. From there business spread in fits and starts, ultimately to London and Manchester in England and beyond.

Economics got its moniker as "the dismal science" when economists in general, and Thomas Malthus[155] in particular, foresaw nothing but continued poverty with population growth exceeding economic growth even as the Industrial Revolution began. Adam Smith,[156] on the other hand, got the point early on. Free enterprise invokes the division and specialization of labor to enhance productivity, allowing substantial numbers of people to escape the poverty trap. Falling birth rates in England as per capita incomes rose created a virtuous circle in the form of a positive feedback loop. Greater productivity generated higher economic growth rates, which in turn drove down population growth rates. As child labor became less important to family survival, families started having fewer

---

154   World Bank. *Doing Business 2018: Reforming to Create Jobs.* Washington, DC: World Bank. doi:10.596/978-1-4648-1146-3. License: Creative Commons Attribution CC by 3.0 IGO.

155   Malthus, T. R. *An Essay on the Principle of Population.* 1798.

156   Smith, Adam. *An Inquiry into the Nature and Causes of the Wealth of Nations.* Printed for Thomas Dobson, at the stone house in Second Street, 1789.

children. A similar story has played out in other developed nations, and it's playing out today in the emerging market countries.

Just as the power of ideas can liberate a people from poverty, such power can enslave them. We are still suffering from the misconceptions of some baby boomers throughout the world. In the eyes of some people, the post–World War II Soviet Union was a progressive society seeking justice and prosperity for its least-advantaged citizens. In their formative years, some people embraced the Soviet story of fairness and equality along with its short-term technological achievements. Soviet leader Nikita Khrushchev created Patrice Lumumba Peoples' Friendship University in Moscow in 1960 to encourage Third World students to come to the Soviet Union for their higher education, where they could be subjected to Soviet propaganda. After the Soviet Union appeared to prove its system superior by winning the 1960 Olympics and getting ahead of the United States in the space race, Western countries that today are relatively pro-business gave aid to antibusiness, nonaligned socialist countries. Around that time the budgets of the African socialist countries Ghana and Uganda became more than 50 percent dependent on Western aid.[157] Their goal was to prevent the nonaligned countries from joining the Soviet countries in the growing anti-Western alliance of socialist countries. The success of the Soviet *Sputnik* (satellite)[158] and related feats of technological prowess deceived many Westerners into thinking that the Soviet way was the wave of the future.

In Africa the pro-socialist mind-set among older Africans is still evident. For some people, free enterprise is still seen as just a vestige of

157   Maraniss, David. *Rome 1960: The Summer Olympics That Stirred the World.* Simon and Schuster, 2009.

158   Launius, Roger, John Logsdon, and Robert Smith (editors). *Reconsidering* Sputnik: *Forty Years Since the Soviet Satellite.* London: Routledge, 2002.

foreign domination and imperialist exploitation. It is no surprise that they have welcomed China's investments, which come with China's policy of no interference in a nation's internal affairs. Moreover, China itself was also a victim of the imperialist powers. Westerners promoting business enterprise as the only true path to prosperity are viewed with suspicion by some older leaders, who see their own power threatened by the unfettered expansion of the business class.

After World War II, Britain and France elected leadership that was wary of returning to unfettered capitalism because of the economic suffering between the two world wars. They were somewhat sympathetic to socialist ideals and turned over key industries to government ownership or oversight.

From the point of view of national and international aid agencies, as well as private nongovernmental aid organizations (NGOs), it was much easier to distribute aid money to national socialist governments with five-year plans than to try to figure out how to distribute money and other resources directly to people in need within those countries. Even where aid resources were not diverted, corruption in high places ensured that government officials receiving aid money could obtain bribes and payoffs for its distribution.

Professors Hubbard and Duggan note that the Marshall Plan has been commonly misunderstood in that it provided aid to businesses much more directly than most people realize. The mistaken belief that the Marshall Plan just provided relief supplies and built roads, bridges, ports, and other infrastructure is well established in some people's minds. In fact, Hubbard and Duggan argue that the funds from the Marshall Plan were given first to local businesses. When the businesses succeeded and paid back the loans to local governments, those governments, in turn, then used the funds to build infrastructure. The professors argue that European revival was more a matter of developing businesses first and adding infrastructure later. Without an expanding local business sector, the revival of Western Europe as a stalwart for democracy in fending off the Russians may well have been a failure. Lifting Europe out of poverty was due primarily to the revival of business.

In *The Aid Trap*, authors Hubbard and Duggan offer local business development under free enterprise as an alternative to pure socialism and National Socialism as in Nazism. They propose an Economic Cooperation Administration to promote local businesses in a manner similar to the Marshall Plan. Freeing Africa from poverty can come about only by freeing businesses from the undue burdens of excessive taxation and regulation and their accompanying corruption requiring myriad bribes and payoffs. When local businesses are free to grow, African countries can finally follow the developed countries and emerging nations out of poverty.

TO PROMOTE CAPITALISM AND ENHANCE OUR SOFT POWER, GO TO KIVA.ORG

Our rich cultural diversity provides us with the enormous potential to use our soft power to influence the world. Our uniquely diverse country has an African component that can speak convincingly to Africans, a Latin component that can speak convincingly to Latin Americans, an Asian component that can speak convincingly to Asians, a European component that can speak convincingly to Europeans, et cetera. Yet within our borders, we speak freely to one another without the intense cultural isolationism, hostility, and antagonisms that are so often evident elsewhere in the world.

For better or worse, humans have always been more trusting of members of their own clan or tribe. America is the clan of clans and tribe of tribes. Our diversity empowers us to bridge the gaps and great divides among the nations of the world. It is not just our military might that sets us apart, but our inclusiveness. To use an old cliché, "We are them and they are us."

In some respects, we provide a mirror image of the world that whets the appetite of our young people to learn more. We have never had a generation more eager to explore the world than today's younger generation. Still in their twenties, they are often considerably more traveled than their parents and grandparents. In contrast to previous generations, they are much more likely to have an ethnically diverse set of friends. In this respect, we are different from much of the rest of the world, which largely remains ethnically divided.

In an attempt to bridge this divide, the European Union has demonstrated the enormous economic and cultural benefits of bringing together a diversity of cultures and languages, not to subsume them but to celebrate them. We should appreciate the value of this approach and take the lead in bringing the world together.

As discussed earlier, each of us can play a small role in bringing the world together through economics. You can start by going to www.kiva.org and loaning a small (or large) bit of money to the budding entrepreneur of your choice.[159] My wife and I loaned $25 to a woman in Togo in Africa who needed $1,200 to buy a freezer to enable her to add fish to her array of local produce for sale in her small grocery store. In less than 48 hours she was fully funded by us and other donors, and over the next year she paid us all back in full. We then loaned that same $25 to three women in Pakistan for their entrepreneurial projects. They, too, paid us back in full within a year.

If you prefer to promote the entrepreneurial spirit right here in your

---

159   See www.kiva.org or www.rotarianmicrocredit.org.

own backyard, you will be glad to know that Kiva has now added small-scale American entrepreneurs to its list of potential loan recipients. If you believe in capitalism, put your money where your mouth is. Loan some money to promote the cause around the world or right here at home.

FREEDOM AND DEMOCRACY IN CHINA

As already noted, world history has displayed two different freedoms: external freedom (freedom from foreign domination) and internal freedom (democracy). People tend to sacrifice internal freedom whenever they are subjected to external threats.

Dictators and quasi-dictators from Fidel Castro (Cuba) and Hugo Chavez (Venezuela) to Kim Jong Il (North Korea) and Recep Tayyip Erdogan (Turkey) have thrived on this effect. Even in the United States, when we felt threatened after 9/11, we gave up personal freedoms by allowing more surveillance, including government wiretapping and data collection. We did this in spite of the fact that since the American Revolution, we have never been subjected to foreign domination. Author Fareed Zakaria has analyzed America's use of its power, especially after the fall of the Soviet Union, where we at first proceeded cautiously under President George H. W. Bush, but then became less careful in using our political, economic, and military power throughout the world.[160]

China has a different history. In the 19th and early 20th centuries, key parts of China were subjugated by a variety of colonial powers. In the late 1930s and early 1940s, China suffered enormously under brutal domination by the Japanese military. Do we really want to be viewed

---

160   Zakaria, Fareed. *The Post-American World*. New York: W. W. Norton & Company, 2009.

as just another country trying to bully China by telling it what to do? During World War II, Chinese peasants rescued our pilots at the risk of the Japanese military wiping out entire Chinese villages in retaliation. We needed each other's friendship then, and we need it now.

China lives in a hostile and unstable region of the world. When a North Korean submarine torpedoed a South Korean warship, the South Koreans cut off trade relations with North Korea. The North Koreans threatened all-out war.[161] A while back a Russian warship sank a Chinese cargo ship after a disagreement over a rice shipment. Eight Chinese crewmen were declared missing and presumed dead.[162] China needs our friendship, and we need China's. Let's be China's friend, not their enemy.

China could have taken the money earned by selling us their products at a discount (favorable exchange rate) and used it to build lots of warships and armaments. Instead China reinvested most of that money back into America via its sovereign wealth funds.[163] When Bath Iron Works in Bath, Maine, needed a 750-foot, 28,000-ton dry dock for building our most advanced guided missile destroyers, China's Jiangdu Yuchai Shipbuilding Company built it for us for $27 million.[164]

Some commentators have referred to our interdependent economies

161   See https://nationalinterest.org/blog/the-buzz/2010-north-korea-sank-south-kore-an-warship-40-sailors-died-24729.

162   Spencer, Richard. "Russian Navy Accused of Sinking Chinese Cargo Ship." The Telegraph. February 19, 2009. https://www.telegraph.co.uk/news/worldnews/asia/china/4697845/Russian-navy-accused-of-sinking-Chinese-cargo-ship.html.

163   Chance, Giles. China and the Credit Crisis. Chichester, UK: John Wiley & Sons, 2010.

164   Hoey, Dennis. "A Behemoth Finesses Its Way into Port." Portland Press Herald. February 17, 2001.

as *Chimerica*.[165] We need to continue building a strong partnership with China and not foolishly undermine it.[166]

Internally China went through the trauma of the Cultural Revolution. Chairman Mao incited young people to rise up against all educated people. Many Chinese leaders today have parents, grandparents, or other relatives who were abused, tortured, or murdered. Some are survivors of imprisonment and abuse themselves. Fear of foreign domination and internal turmoil is not just a concern of the Chinese leadership but also of the Chinese people themselves.

Throughout American history we have been able to completely "overthrow" our own government via the ballot box. We have been able to change presidents without spilling even a few crumbs at the preinaugural White House coffee. Not every country is so fortunate. Widespread riots and turmoil in China are in no one's interest.

China may not be a democracy in the European or American sense, but it is not a brutal dictatorship. No doubt people have been held without a fair trial, just as we have done at Guantánamo. No doubt some have been abused, as we did at Abu Ghraib. The best thing we can do to encourage other countries to respect human rights is to actually respect human rights ourselves.

Ultimately, the Chinese people will determine in their own way if and when they are ready for a full democracy of the people, by the people, and for the people. If our government tries to force its own views on China, it will only rally the Chinese people around their government

---

165   Ferguson, Niall. *The Ascent of Money*. New York: Penguin Press, 2008.

166   Karabell, Zachary. *Superfusion: How China and America Became One Economy*. New York: Simon and Schuster, 2009.

and motivate them to sacrifice more internal freedom to maintain their external independence.[167]

DOES TRADE WITH CHINA THREATEN AMERICAN JOBS?

It is interesting that our politicians want Americans to be angry with the Chinese for offering their products at prices that are too low. The Chinese used their natural resources and the hard work of their people to produce products for us. Instead of sending them an equivalent quantity of our products, we sent them pieces of paper with George Washington's picture on it. Who is getting ripped off here? It is not us.

Is it in America's best interest to raise prices in Walmart and other discount stores where most Americans shop, or should we keep prices low and direct our country toward the knowledge-based jobs of the 21st century? Some have claimed that we will never be able to compete with China with its low-wage workers, even as shortages of such workers in China began to emerge just prior to the recent recession. China in turn has been losing out to low-wage workers in Vietnam and other Southeast Asian countries. African countries no doubt will eventually take their turn in taking possession of low-wage jobs.

China has already figured this out and is moving to raise the knowledge intensity and quality of its products and the education of its people. American politicians like to claim that they are the ones who will protect American jobs from "unfair" foreign competition. James Buchanan received the Nobel Prize in economics in 1986 for

---

167   Zakaria, Fareed. *The Future of Freedom.* New York: W. W. Norton & Company, 2003, explains how economic reforms in China do not guarantee political reform, yet liberalization in China may determine the fate of the world.

his work in public choice theory, in which he implies that those who are likely to lose their jobs to imports have an intense personal interest in voting and lobbying to block imports, while all the voters who benefit slightly from the lower prices provided by those imports have much less motivation to vote or lobby in support of blocking foreign competition. The majority who would benefit from lower prices remain silent, while a minority who would lose their jobs lobby intensely to block foreign competition.

Foreign competition is only "unfair" in taking away jobs by offering better-quality products at lower prices if there are a fixed number of jobs. As previously noted, economists know this idea as the lump of labor fallacy—that the number of jobs is finite. In reality, the number and quality of jobs is very dynamic and determined by the forces of supply and demand. Fiscal and monetary policies contribute to new demand along with rising export demand. New demand is being generated all the time for new products that didn't even exist in the 20th century. The problem is that old workers are trained in old, unskilled jobs or skilled jobs like welding or forklift operations—which are becoming automated as computers take over in manufacturing. Manufacturing *production* isn't declining in America, but manufacturing *employment* is, in the face of "lights-out" manufacturing where robots work through the night with no complaints and few breaks.[168] Many of the jobs going to China would have gone to robots here in the United States anyway. The jobs going to China, then on to Vietnam, and then on to Africa are just stopping briefly on their way to oblivion, because most of those jobs will end up losing out to automation no matter where they land.

---

168   Boreham, Paul, Rachel Parker, Paul Thompson, and Robert Hall. *New Technology @ Work*. London: Routledge, 2008.

If you want job security in the 21st century, don't learn welding. Instead, learn what a relational database is. Learn a computer programming language. Learn how to use sampling to estimate the probability of an unlikely event. Learn how to create and use a collaborative filter. Learn what a Taylor series expansion is. Learn how to put together a business plan and how to determine if a business process is scalable or not scalable. These basics and many more can be learned on your own through a Google search. Some of what you need to know to compete in the 21st century can be found on Wikipedia and/or YouTube.

China's old guard leadership came from the engineering class. They understand all this. They know these low-wage manufacturing jobs are a flash in the pan that won't last. They are preparing China for the 21st century.

SUMMARY, OVERVIEW, AND TRANSITION

This chapter examined the important role of money flow in international trade and investments to establish and maintain efficient resource allocation across the world. In particular, a generous win-win approach has served the United States and the world well in reviving Germany and Japan immediately after World War II, in supporting Mexico in the mid-1990s, and in dealing with China and other trading partners today.

We have all benefited from the law of comparative advantage through the division of labor in providing high-quality products at lower prices. Policies that block trade through the use of tariffs and other means interfere with money flow and are generally shortsighted and not in the national interest. Insisting on a "balanced trade" between any two countries is like insisting that you earn enough money working for Walmart to pay for what you buy at Walmart. It makes no sense. There are countries that buy our exports, while we do not import anything from them. Conversely, there are countries that produce products we import, but we do not export anything to them. This is normal, reasonable, and *not* a problem.

International aid can be helpful when it goes directly to supporting business, but it can be counterproductive when reinforcing corrupt regimes and natural resource dependency. With globalization the economic stability of any individual country is to an ever-increasing degree dependent upon the economic well-being of other countries.

CHAPTER 9

SUMMARY: CREATING OPTIMAL MONEY FLOW FOR A HEALTHY ECONOMY

Technological progress has meant an increase in fixed cost relative to variable cost. Machines and computer code replace workers and decision makers. Why pay a human a lot of money in variable costs when you can just replace that employee with a more or less one-time payment for a robot or an algorithm? Variable cost falls from a salary with benefits to a few drops of oil now and then to the equipment or an occasional tweak to the computer code.[169]

---

169 In production, an average hour of machine time produces significantly more value than an average hour of human time. Consequently, if one assumes diminishing marginal productivity, equating the value of their marginal products per dollar requires a lot more machine time relative to human time.

As the return to labor has slowed with the decline in variable costs, the return to investments in physical, digital, and human capital has increased as fixed costs have come to dominate our economy. Advances in technology have brought about large-scale job losses in manufacturing, such as with the widespread use of robotics in the automotive industry. Brick-and-mortar retail businesses are losing jobs to Amazon and other internet direct-delivery systems; driverless trucks threaten to replace 3.5 million truck drivers in the United States. Advances in artificial intelligence may eliminate many legal, medical, and financial jobs. We must help people make the move from old, out-of-date jobs to new, up-to-date jobs by offering vocational retraining. Because the return to capital has become so much greater than the return to labor, one does not need a PhD in finance to realize that the goal over one's career is to make the transition from getting your money from labor to getting your money from capital. Retirement completes this transition.

COGNITIVE CAPTURE GIVES LOBBYISTS POLITICAL POWER

We have seen, in addition to technological change, a fundamental shift in political power away from the general population and into the hands of special interests. Lobbying has enabled large campaign contributors to get special access to politicians and gain special advantages and influence through *cognitive capture*. Lobbyists gain this access so they can try to convince lawmakers that the lobbyists' special interests should be written into the law. Lobbyists have written many laws and regulations to their own advantage. "The Art of the Deal" has become "the Art of the Tax Loophole," such as with IRC-469 limiting special tax depreciation write-offs to those with enough properties requiring at least 750 hours of property management during any given tax year, and with IRC-482 that allows for transferring costs overseas to tax shelters.

With the return to capital being much greater than the return to labor, a greater and greater percentage of the money flow has been directed toward those with the lowest marginal propensity to consume—the wealthy. With longer life expectancy and lower birth rates, there has been a dramatic decline in the labor force relative to the number of retirees. These fundamental shifts in our economy have distorted the money flow and hindered the growth of our economy. With fewer jobs and fewer workers, our GDP may well shrink rather than grow in real terms (and prices will rise), unless immigration provides us with a younger, more dynamic workforce.

ECONOMIC INEQUALITY LEADS TO ECONOMIC INSTABILITY

Economic inequality leads to insufficient money flow to the lower and middle classes. In the absence of adequate money flow, generating enough demand for goods and services to keep the economy running at full capacity while keeping unemployment low requires a slowly growing *consumer debt bubble*, where the majority of consumers gradually slide deeper and deeper into debt. To keep the economy going, Republicans promote tax cuts while Democrats promote infrastructure spending, which both contribute to a *federal debt bubble* to try to make up for insufficient money flow to the middle and lower classes.

At the same time, a great deal of money flows to several large corporations with monopoly or oligopoly power and to the wealthy top 1 percent, thus creating a *massive savings bubble*. The wealthy, who already possess enough money to have whatever goods and services they want, use the extra money that flows to them to purchase stocks and bonds, mortgage-backed securities, collateral debt obligations, and other financial products and derivatives. The largest corporations use the excessive money flowing their way to consolidate their power by purchasing potential rivals and buying back their own stock.[170] These forces drive stock prices up to unsustainable levels.[171]

The massive savings of the wealthy overwhelms credit markets, keeping real interest rates too low to entice sufficient investment to keep the economy at full employment without the help of a growing lower- and middle-class consumer debt bubble. In other words, extreme economic inequality leads to a *permanent Keynesian liquidity trap*, with the consumer debt bubble, the federal debt bubble, and stock market bubble allowed to grow until they burst.

Economic inequality inevitably leads to economic instability.

FISCAL POLICY TO PROVIDE MONEY FLOW TO MIDDLE CLASS

One possible solution to the continued buildup of such bubble economies is taxation to divert the money flow to the lower and middle classes through government programs such as better health care, more infrastructure spending, higher teacher pay, better and more widely shared educational opportunities, et cetera. Rather than encouraging business expansion, the "starve the beast" mantra of severely limiting the size of government restricts government expenditures, resulting in a less healthy business environment. More often than not, government expenditures stimulate ("crowd in") rather than "crowd out" business activity. Government expenditures often serve as the grease that keeps

---

170   Foroohar, Rana. *Makers and Takers*. New York: Penguin Random House, 2017, provides a more detailed discussion of stock buybacks and their consequences.

171   Pearlstein, Steven. *Can American Capitalism Survive?* New York: St. Martin's Press, 2018, explains how the single-minded focus on shareholder value has undermined the stability and health of the American economy.

business wheels spinning—rather than as a substitute for business activity. They also spur innovative breakthroughs such as the internet, GPS, and many other contributions to basic research through the National Institutes of Health and the National Science Foundation, all benefits that would not come from businesses focused on maximizing their stock price. A key aspect of the new money flow paradigm is recognizing the many ways in which government can contribute to the efficient allocation of resources within an economy, and its central role in properly directing money flow to maintain a healthy economy and maximize economic growth and prosperity.

INTERNATIONAL MONEY FLOW LOWERS PRICES FOR ALL

One of the most poorly understood concepts in economics is the balance of trade. Before money was invented, trade was between pairs of individuals. If you wanted a horse, but had a cow, you would have to find someone who was willing to trade their horse for your cow. After money was invented, you could sell to some people but buy from an entirely different set of people. The idea that every pair of countries must have *balanced trade* with neither a surplus nor a deficit is like saying that I must make enough things to sell to Walmart to pay for what I buy at Walmart.

There are 195 countries in the world. We sell our exports to some countries but import nothing from them. We buy imports from some other countries but export nothing to them. Trying to force China or Mexico to maintain a strict balance in our imports and exports to each country makes no sense at all and is damaging to us, as well as to China and Mexico. The whole point of creating money was so we could shop around, buying from some and selling to others. Following a one-on-one balanced trade agenda means going back to one-on-one bartering. I do not know of a single economist, conservative or liberal, who thinks that the one-on-one balanced trade approach makes any sense.

Even an overall trade deficit has its advantages and disadvantages. Consider what happens when the Chinese take their resources and use them to create products for us. In return for these imports from China, instead of sending our own products to them, we send them US dollars. How is this ripping us off? Ordinarily, if a country buys more than it sells, then the excess of its currency in foreign exchange markets causes the value of its currency to decline. This means that the price of that country's exports declines and the price of imports into that country increases, causing exports to rise and imports to fall, and bringing exports and imports back into balance.[172] If we want the value of our currency to decline so our trading partners will buy more from us, we can increase our foreign aid to give more US dollars to the countries that are most likely to buy our exports.

However, China did not let most of the US dollars it received go into the foreign exchange markets, but instead used them to buy US Treasury bonds. China now has well over a trillion dollars in US treasuries. In other words, China invested most of the US dollars it received back into the American economy. Again, how is this ripping us off? We paid China for the imports, but China gave us our money back by buying our Treasury bonds.

Why would China do this? Basically, the answer is that China had an immediate political problem. China faced a flow of people out of the countryside and into the cities. It needed a quick way to employ millions of people. Having them make products for export was a quick solution to

---

172   The failure to achieve balanced trade is in part due to the ever-expanding role of the US dollar as the international reserve currency.

avoid political unrest. More recently, China has been building up a middle class capable of maintaining a substantial domestic demand for goods and services so that it is no longer as dependent on exports to maintain full employment. It can now directly increase middle-class demand.

We've certainly lost a lot of menial jobs to China in this process, mainly in textile manufacturing, although most of our major job losses have been to technology. But the number of jobs in this world is not fixed. With the right economic policies, we can create as many jobs as we want and need.

LUMP OF LABOR FALLACY POSITS FIXED NUMBER OF JOBS

Pretending that there is a fixed number of jobs is known to economists as the *lump of labor fallacy*. A major impediment to job creation has been the fear of inflation based on the *Phillips Curve*, which posits a trade-off between lower unemployment and higher inflation. The Phillips Curve was first proposed by New Zealand economist William Phillips in a 1958 article in the journal *Economica*.[173] This trade-off seems to have been operative during the 1970s and 1980s, but since sometime in the 1990s it has no longer worked.

In the past, wealthy individuals with political power were afraid that excessively low unemployment would lead to inflation. They felt that a reserve army of the unemployed was necessary to keep labor costs down and avoid inflation. More recently, they have seen inflation as less likely

---

173   Phillips, A. W. "The Relationship between Unemployment and the Rate of Change of Money Wages in the United Kingdom 1861–1957." *Economica*, Vol. 25, No. 100 (1958): 283–299.

due to automation and globalization, and have allowed policies that promote full employment and economic growth.

Foreign trade is not about jobs, because we can increase or decrease jobs with policies that increase or decrease demand for goods and services. Foreign trade is really about prices, where a tariff is, in effect, a sales tax imposed on goods produced abroad. A tariff handicaps competition from abroad and allows domestic firms to raise prices. In the 19th century, Great Britain unilaterally removed its own tariffs when it realized that it could get better-quality goods at lower prices by not taxing goods from overseas. More recently, South Korea and Chile have unilaterally removed their tariffs for the same reason.

If another country wants to shoot itself in the foot by allowing special interests to get their politicians to discourage or block products from abroad, that is their prerogative. Imposing a discriminatory sales tax in the form of a tariff is not in our national interest. If other countries wish to raise the prices their citizens have to pay for goods and services, let them. But imposing tariffs on imports into the United States just increases the prices that our consumers must pay. Full employment does not require tariffs.

CONCLUSION

Money flows through the economy as blood flows through the body. Just as a healthy body requires that blood flow to all of its parts, a healthy economy requires keeping money flowing to all economic sectors and income classes. The money flow paradigm recognizes the inherent dysfunctionality of unsupervised free market economy and the essential role of government in the efficient allocation of resources. Previous economic paradigms treated government as an outside alien force with a very limited role to play in economic efficiency and stability. The money flow paradigm sees government as the heart of the free enterprise system.

Both the natural transition from a labor-intensive economy to a more capital-intensive economy and the ever-increasing political influence of special interests have changed our economy to direct most of the money flow to the wealthiest individuals and largest corporations. Consequently, the federal government is pressured to use deficit spending to augment consumer demand so the middle class can afford to buy back the goods and services that it produces. This distorted money flow has created a *consumer debt bubble* for the middle class, a *massive savings bubble* for the wealthy, and a *federal debt bubble* for us all. This triple bubble undermines the stability of our economy by creating and maintaining a *permanent Keynesian liquidity trap* in which real interest rates get trapped at close to zero when nominal interest rates more or less match the inflation rate. Any attempt by the Fed to raise interest rates to normal or "neutral" levels threatens to push the economy into recession.

Cryptocurrencies threaten to replace dollars with purely digital money. The Fed needs to offer a new digital money system that enables consumers to make direct phone-to-phone money transfers to pay for the purchase of goods and services (e.g., M-Pesa in Kenya).

Up until now our Federal Reserve has had to raise or lower interest rates by selling or buying Treasury securities, with effects that only gradually make it from the financial markets to the broader economy. Such a lagged response to economic conditions is like driving a car and having a long lag from the time you turn the steering wheel to the time the car turns. Say a deer jumps out in front of your car. You instantly turn the steering wheel to try to miss the deer, but because of that lagged response, your wheels don't turn for 20 seconds. It should be no surprise that such a car would crash from time to time. Likewise, the economy can fall into recession before the Fed's actions are able to turn things around.

Moreover, the sellers of those Treasury securities typically use the Fed's money to buy stocks or other financial products so there is little, if any, increase in the demand for consumer products and services. A new approach is needed to give the Federal Reserve more direct and immediate control over consumer demand for goods and services in our economy.

Historically, government-issued dollars have dominated business transactions in the United States, but new cryptocurrencies are beginning to offer an alternative currency beyond the control of the Federal Reserve. These cryptocurrencies allow criminals, such as drug dealers, to secretly transfer large amounts of cash outside the Federal Reserve System.

The Federal Reserve needs a new policy tool where everyone aged 18 and older with a Social Security number is automatically given a "My America" prosperity account with the Federal Reserve Bank. This would allow the Federal Reserve direct access to the consumer and give it the ability to steer the economy away from an imminent recession. Just as the Federal Reserve creates money when it buys Treasury securities, the money injected into the "My America" prosperity accounts would not require additional taxes and would not add to the national debt. Individuals could use their smartphones to transfer money from their "My America" prosperity account to another person's individual prosperity account to pay for anything they might want to purchase. Interest could be earned on only the first $10,000 to avoid disrupting the commercial banking system. This restriction would enable commercial banks to retain the largest, most profitable accounts while losing the smallest, costliest checking accounts. Gradually, and before too long, these "My America" smartphone accounts will replace the old-fashioned paper checking accounts that have been used so widely in the 20th century.

Such accounts could also be used to prevent inflation. The whole point of the existence of interest rates is to delay consumption. When excessive inflation threatens, the Federal Reserve could raise the inter-est rate on the accounts and increase the annual limit on individual account contributions to withdraw money from the economy and reduce inflationary pressure. This would be in addition to the usual anti-inflation strategy of the Fed selling Treasury securities in New York financial markets.

We will continue to suffer from unnecessary slack in our economy and occasional recessions until we realize that our current system is too slow in responding to the economic distortions and disruptions that develop from our unbalanced money flow.

Individual "My America" prosperity accounts will enable us to directly and immediately control consumer demand for goods and services with-out an excessive and unnecessary time lag. Initially, the Federal Reserve Bank would put $1,000 into each "My America" prosperity account, which could not be withdrawn. However, any interest earned could be withdrawn at any time along with any additional money injected into the account by the Federal Reserve when demand for goods and services was lagging and recession threatened. The interest earned in these accounts would be tax-free. The IRS would also deposit tax refunds into the indi-vidual accounts. Consumers could deposit money up to an annual limit or withdraw money from their account using their smartphone with triple authentication, including face recognition, and preregistration of their phone or internet device along with a secure personal password.[174]

By setting up these individual accounts and improving econometric models that track the economy—by combining the standard models used by experts (known professionally as dynamic stochastic general equilibrium models) with the pattern recognition models used in artificial intelligence, such as hierarchal hidden Markov models, artificial neural network models, and/or multidimensional spline regression models, et cetera—the Federal Reserve could keep the economy permanently at full employment and at the same time avoid excessive inflation.

In conclusion, this book offers a new paradigm for redefining the role of government and understanding the effects of our extreme income and wealth inequality in terms of the triple bubbles of *consumer debt, wealthy savings,* and *federal debt.* It explains how these factors have created a *permanent liquidity trap* and what can be done to more directly and immediately control consumer demand to maintain a healthy and robust full-employment economy without relying on unpaid-for tax cuts and excessive government expenditures.

Most importantly, the new money flow paradigm calls for altering monetary policy in response to economic downturns to inject money directly into the economy through "My America" prosperity accounts

---

174   Each account holder's smartphone, laptop computer, desktop computer, and any other internet connectivity device could be registered and blockchained together with the user's Federal Reserve account. A unique algorithm would be installed on the user's internet device, with that same algorithm installed at the user's account at the Federal Reserve Bank. With device preregistration, face recognition, and a secure personal password, the algorithm would generate a unique 60-digit alphanumeric password that would change with each transaction. The user would not be aware of this longer password, but it would prevent any third party from capturing and reusing that 60-digit password. This would ensure the security of each user's "My America" prosperity account.

instead of encouraging more indebtedness by lowering interest rates. More generally, the money flow paradigm at last appreciates government's central role in guiding the economy and enhancing economic efficiency at both the microeconomic and macroeconomic levels.

REFERENCES

Abbott, Chuck. "Trump Proposes 33% Cut in Crop Insurance."
    Successful Farming at Agriculture.com. February 13,
    2018. https://www.agriculture.com/news/business/
    trump-proposes-33-cut-in-crop-insurance.

Aharony, Joseph, and Itzhak Swary. "Contagion Effects of Bank
    Failures." *The Journal of Business*, Vol. 56, No. 3 (1983): 305–322.

Akerlof, George A. "The Market for 'Lemons': Quality Uncertainty and
    the Market Mechanism." *Quarterly Journal of Economics*, Vol. 84,
    No. 3 (1970): 488–500. doi:10.2307/1879431.

Anderson, Kaila. "Free Market Meets Altruism in Kiva." *The Orange
    County Register*. March 12, 2010.

Ariely, Dan. *Predictably Irrational*. New York: HarperCollins, 2008.

Associated Press. "Tons of Food Aid Rotting in Haiti Ports." *Barbados
    Free Press*. March 7, 2008.

Auerbach, Alan J., and Daniel Feenberg. "The Significance of Federal
    Taxes as Automatic Stabilizers." *Journal of Economic Perspectives*,
    Vol. 14, No. 3 (2000): 37–56.

Baumol, William J. *The Cost Disease: Why Computers Get Cheaper and
    Health Care Doesn't*. New Haven, CT: Yale University Press, 2012.

Becker, Gary. *Human Capital: A Theoretical and Empirical Analysis, with Special Reference to Education.* Chicago: University of Chicago Press, 1964.

Beddoes, Zanny Minton, et al. *Debts, Deficits and Dilemmas.* London: Profile Books, Ltd., 2014.

Berentsen, Aleksander, and Fabian Schär. "The Case for Central Bank Electronic Money and the Non-Case for Central Bank Cryptocurrencies." *Federal Reserve Bank of St. Louis Review,* Vol. 100, No. 2 (2018): 97–106.

Bernanke, Ben S., Timothy F. Geithner, and Henry M. Paulson Jr. *Firefighting: The Financial Crisis and Its Lessons.* New York: Penguin Random House, 2019.

Biewen, Martin, Bernd Fitzenberger, and Jakob de Lazzer. "The Role of Employment Interruptions and Part-Time Work for the Rise in Wage Inequality." *IZA Journal of Labor Economics,* Vol. 7, No. 1 (2018): 1–34.

Bivens, Josh, Lawrence Mishel, and John Schmitt. *It's Not Just Monopoly and Monopsony: How Market Power Has Affected American Wages.* Washington, DC: Economic Policy Institute, April 2018.

Blanchard, Olivier. "Should We Reject the Natural Rate Hypothesis?" Working Paper. Peterson Institute for International Economics and Massachusetts Institute of Technology, version 2.0. November 21, 2017.

Blyth, Mark, and Eric Lonergan. "Print Less but Transfer More: Why Central Banks Should Give Money Directly to the People." *Foreign Affairs,* Vol. 93 (September/October 2014).

Boreham, Paul, Rachel Parker, Paul Thompson, and Robert Hall. *New Technology @ Work.* London: Routledge, 2008.

Brafman, Ori, and Rom Brafman. *Sway: The Irresistible Pull of Irrational Behavior.* New York: Random House, 2009.

Bremmer, Ian. *Us versus Them: The Failure of Globalism*. New York: Penguin Random House, 2018.

Brill, Steven. *Tailspin: The People and Forces behind America's Fifty-Year Fall—And Those Trying to Reverse It*. New York: Alfred F. Knopf, 2018.

Brooks, David. *Bobos in Paradise*. New York: Simon and Schuster, 2000.

Bullough, Oliver. *Moneyland*. London: Profile Books, Ltd., 2018.

Camerer, C. F., George Loewenstein, and Mathew Rabin (editors). *Advances in Behavioral Economics*. Princeton, NJ: Princeton University Press, 2004.

Carroll, Christopher, Jiri Slacalek, Kiici Tokuoka, and Matthew N. White. "The Distribution of Wealth and the Marginal Propensity to Consume." *Quantitative Economics*, No. 8 (2017): 977–1020.

Cengiz, Doruk, Arindrajit Dube, Attila Lindner, and Ben Zipperer. "The Effect of Minimum Wages on the Total Number of Jobs: Evidence from the United States using a Bunching Estimator." Working Paper. April 30, 2017.

Chance, Giles. *China and the Credit Crisis*. Hoboken, NJ: John Wiley & Sons, 2010.

Clifford, Steven. *The CEO Pay Machine*. New York: Penguin Random House, 2017.

Cooper, George. *Fixing Economics*. Hampshire: Harriman House Ltd., 2016.

———. *Money, Blood and Revolution*. Hampshire: Harriman House Ltd., 2014.

———. *The Origin of Financial Crises*. New York: Vintage, 2008.

Dalio, Ray. *Principles for Navigating BIG DEBT CRISES*. Westport, CT: Bridgewater Associates, LLP, 2018.

Deneen, Patrick J. *Why Liberalism Failed*. New Haven, CT: Yale University Press, 2018.

Dickens, Charles. *Bleak House*. London: Bradbury & Evans, 1853.

Dixon, Peter B., and Maureen T. Rimmer. "The Dependence of US Employment on Canada, 2013." Centre of Policy Studies at Victoria University, 2014. https://www.copsmodels.com/pdf/canada_trade_2013.pdf.

Duchin, Moon. "Geometry v. Gerrymandering." *Scientific American*, Vol. 319, No. 5 (November 2018): 49–53.

"The Dutch Disease." *The Economist*. November 26, 1977.

Ferguson, Niall. *The Ascent of Money*. New York: Penguin Press, 2008.

Fisher, Irving. "The Debt-Deflation Theory of Great Depressions." *Econometrica*, Vol. 1, No. 4 (1933): 337–357.

Foroohar, Rana. *Makers and Takers*. New York: Penguin Random House, 2017.

Friedman, Milton. *The Optimum Quantity of Money*. New Brunswick, NJ: Aldine Transaction, 2007.

Friedman, Thomas L. *Hot, Flat, and Crowded*. New York: Picador, 2009.

Geanakopolos, John. "Three Brief Proofs of Arrow's Impossibility Theorem." *Economic Theory*, Vol. 26, No. 1 (July 2005): 211–215.

Gore, Al. *An Inconvenient Truth*. New York: Rodale, 2006.

Haass, Richard. *A World in Disarray*. New York: Penguin Random House, 2017.

Harari, Yuval Noah. *Homo Deus*. New York: HarperCollins, 2016.

———. *Sapiens*. Tel Aviv: Kinneret, Zmora-Bitan, Dvir., 2011.

Harvey, William. *On the Motion of the Heart and Blood in Animals*. Frankfurt, 1628.

Heckman, James J. "Sample Selection Bias as a Specification Error." *Econometrica*, Vol. 47, No. 1 (1979): 153–61. doi:10.2307/1912352. JSTOR 1912352. MR 0518832.

Heller, Michael. *The Gridlock Economy*. New York: Basic Books, 2008.

Hirsch, Fred. *Social Limits to Growth*. Cambridge, MA: Harvard University Press, 1976.

Hoey, Dennis. "A Behemoth Finesses Its Way into Port." *Portland Press Herald*. February 17, 2001.

Hollander, Samuel. *The Economics of Thomas Robert Malthus*. Toronto: University of Toronto Press, 1997.

Hubbard, Glenn, and William Duggan. *The Aid Trap*. New York: Columbia University Press, 2009.

Jardin, Ekaterina, Mark C. Long, Robert Plotnick, Emma van Inwegen, Jacob Vigor, and Hilary Wething. "Minimum Wage Increases, Wages, and Low-Wage Employment: Evidence from Seattle." NBER Working Paper No. 23532. October 2017.

Kahneman, Daniel. *Thinking Fast and Slow*. New York: Farrar, Straus & Giroux, 2011.

Karabell, Zachary. *Superfusion: How China and America Became One Economy*. New York: Simon and Schuster, 2009.

Kinsley, Michael. *Creative Capitalism*. New York: Simon and Schuster, 2008.

Kleiner, M. M., and Alan Krueger. "Analyzing the Extent and Influence of Occupational Licensing on the Labor Market." *Journal of Labor Economics*, Vol. 31, No. 2 (2013): S173–S202.

Krugman, Paul R. "It's Baaack: Japan's Slump and the Return of the Liquidity Trap." *Brookings Papers on Economic Activity*, No. 2 (1998): 137–205.

———. *End This Depression Now!* New York: W. W. Norton & Company, 2012.

Launius, Roger, John Logsdon, and Robert Smith (editors). *Reconsidering* Sputnik: *Forty Years Since the Soviet Satellite*. London: Routledge, 2002.

Levy, Michael. "Why $30 a Barrel Oil Could Save Lives, Bring

Democracy to Iran and End the War" (Op-Ed). *News Blaze.* July 10, 2009.

Locke, John. *Two Treatises of Government.* London: Awnsham Churchill, 1689.

Lucas, Robert. "Expectations and the Neutrality of Money." *Journal of Economic Theory*, Vol. 4, No. 2 (1972).

Malthus, T. R. *An Essay on the Principle of Population.* 1798.

Mankiw, Gregory, and Ricardo Reis. "Sticky Information versus Sticky Prices: A Proposal to Replace the New Keynesian Phillips Curve." *Quarterly Journal of Economics*, Vol. 117, No. 4 (2002): 1295–1328.

Maraniss, David. *Rome 1960: The Summer Olympics That Stirred the World.* New York: Simon and Schuster, 2009.

"Mark Zuckerberg's Commencement Address at Harvard." *The Harvard Gazette.* May 25, 2017. http://news.harvard.edu/gazette/story/2017/05/mark-zuckerbergs-speech-as-written-for-harvards-class-of-2017/.

Marsh, Lawrence C., and Meredith Scovill. "Evaluating the Future of a Self-Financed Social Security System." *Modeling and Simulation*, Vol. 9. Proceedings of the 1978 Pittsburgh Simulation Conference, Pittsburgh, Pennsylvania, 1978.

———. "Using System Dynamics to Model the Social Security System." NBER Workshop on Policy Analysis with Social Security Research Files. Williamsburg, Virginia, March 15–17, 1978.

McKay, Alisdair, and Ricardo Reis. "The Role of Automatic Stabilizers in the US Business Cycle." *Econometrica*, Vol. 84, No. 1 (2013): 141–194.

Minsky, Hyman P. *Stabilizing an Unstable Economy.* New Haven, CT: Yale University Press, 1986.

Moyo, Dambisa. *Dead Aid.* New York: Farrar, Straus & Giroux, 2009.

Muth, John F. "Rational Expectations and the Theory of Price Movements." *Econometrica*, Vol. 29 (1961): 315–335.

Nozick, Robert. *Anarchy, State and Utopia*. New York: Basic Books, 1974.

Ostrom, Elinor. *Governing the Commons*. Cambridge: Cambridge University Press, 1990.

Ostry, Jonathan D., Prakash Loungani, and Andrew Berg. *Confronting Inequality: How Societies Can Choose Inclusive Growth*. New York: Columbia University Press, January 2019.

Pearlstein, Steven. *Can American Capitalism Survive?* New York: St. Martin's Press, 2018.

Piketty, Thomas. *Capital in the 21st Century*. Cambridge, MA: Harvard University Press, 2014.

Piketty, Thomas, and Emmanuel Saez. "A Theory of Optimal Inheritance Taxation." *Econometrica*, Vol. 81, No. 5 (September 2013): 1851–1886.

Polk, William R. *Understanding Iran*. New York: Palgrave-Macmillan, 2009.

Ramsey, Valerie A. "Can Government Purchases Stimulate the Economy?" *Journal of Economic Literature*, Vol. 49, No. 3 (2011): 673–685.

Rawls, John. *A Theory of Justice*. Cambridge, MA: Belknap Press, 1971.

Reich, Robert B. *Aftershock: The Next Economy & America's Future*. New York: Vintage Books, 2011.

———. *The Common Good*. New York: Penguin Random House, 2018.

Ricardo, David. *The Principles of Political Economy and Taxation*. J. M. Dent & Sons, 1911.

Ricks, Morgan, John Crawford, and Lev Menand. "A Public Option for Bank Accounts (Or Central Banking for All)." Vanderbilt Law Research Paper 18–33; UC Hastings Research Paper No. 287. June 6, 2018.

Rifkin, Jeremy. *The Zero Marginal Cost Society*. New York: St. Martin's Press, 2014.

Rosen, Sherwin. "The Economics of Superstars." *The American Economic Review*, Vol. 71, No. 5 (December 1981): 845–858.

Schelling, Thomas C. *Micromotives and Macrobehavior*. New York: W. W. Norton & Company, 1978 and 2006.

Schumpeter, Joseph A. *Capitalism, Socialism and Democracy*. New York: Harper & Brothers, 1942.

Schwartz, Barry. *The Paradox of Choice*. New York: HarperCollins, 2004.

Sen, Amartya. *Development as Freedom*. New York: Anchor Books, 1999.

Shermer, M. *The Mind of the Market*. New York: Henry Holt and Company, 2008.

Shiller, Robert. *Narrative Economics: How Stories Go Viral and Drive Major Economic Events*. Princeton, NJ: Princeton University Press, 2019.

Slaughter, Anne-Marie. *The Chessboard and the Web*. New Haven, CT: Yale University Press, 2017.

Smith, Adam. *An Inquiry into the Nature and Causes of the Wealth of Nations*. London: W. Strahan and T. Cadell, 1776.

———. *The Theory of Moral Sentiments*. Edinburgh: Andrew Millar, in the Strand; and Alexander Kincaid and J. Bell, 1759.

Summers, Lawrence H. *The Post-Widget Society: Economic Possibilities for Our Children*. New York: Farrar, Straus & Giroux, 2021.

"System Dynamics." Wikipedia. https://en.wikipedia.org/wiki/System_dynamics.

Taleb, Nassim N. *Antifragile: Things that Gain from Disorder*. New York: Random House, 2014.

———. *The Black Swan: The Impact of the Highly Improbable*. New York: Random House, 2010.

Thaler, Richard H. *Misbehaving: The Making of Behavioral Economics*. New York: W. W. Norton and Company, 2016.

Thaler, Richard H., and Cass R. Sunstein. *Nudge: Improving Decisions about Health, Wealth and Happiness*. New Haven, CT: Yale University Press, 2008.

Tobias, Manuela. "Comparing Administrative Costs for Private Insurance and Medicare." PolitiFact. September 20, 2017. https://www.politifact.com/truth-o-meter/statements/2017/sep/20/bernie-s/comparing-administrative-costs-private-insurance-a/.

Triana, Pablo. *Lecturing Birds on Flying: Can Mathematical Theories Destroy the Financial Markets?* Hoboken, NJ: John Wiley & Sons, 2009.

Ubel, Peter. *Free Market Madness*. Boston: Harvard Business Press, 2009.

Warren, Elizabeth, and Amelia Warren Tyagi. *Two-Income Trap: Why Middle-Class Parents Are Still Going Broke*. New York: Basic Books, 2003 (updated in 2016).

Williamson, Oliver. *The Mechanisms of Governance*. Oxford: Oxford University Press, 1996.

Wolff, Edward N. "Household Wealth Trends in the United States, 1962 to 2016: Has Middle Class Wealth Recovered?" NBER Working Paper No. 24085, November 2017.

World Bank. *Doing Business 2010* (annual report). New York: Palgrave-Macmillan, 2009.

Wren-Lewis, Simon. "Ending the Microfoundations Hegemony."

Oxford Review of Economic Policy, Vol. 34, Nos. 1–2 (January 2018): 55–69. https://doi.org/10.1093/oxrep/grx054.

Wright, Randall. "On the Future of Macro: A New Monetarist Perspective." *Oxford Review of Economic Policy*, Vol. 34, Nos. 1–2 (2018):107–131.

Zakaria, Fareed. *The Future of Freedom*. New York: W. W. Norton & Company, 2003.

———. *The Post-American World*. New York: W. W. Norton & Company, 2009.

Zuckerberg, Mark. "Mark Zuckerberg Harvard Commencement Speech 2017." YouTube. Posted by ABC News. May 25, 2017. https://www.youtube.com/watch?v=QM8l623AouM.

ACKNOWLEDGMENTS

I am grateful to my friends and colleagues from the University of Notre Dame, the University of Chicago, and Avila University for their insights and arguments both for and against the various analyses and policy proposals presented in this book. I am particularly grateful to my former graduate students who made many suggestions for improvements and shared my objective of trying to get people to think more carefully about the issues they cared the most about. I would like to thank the journalists from the *South Bend Tribune* and *The Kansas City Star* who taught me and showed me excellence in journalism. I am especially grateful to Erik Tyler, Elizabeth Brown, and Jeffrey Curry, who went over my manuscript page by page and word by word. They offered many suggestions for improvement but are in no way responsible for any remaining errors of commission or omission.

Many of my former classmates and some of my dearest relatives played a key role in keeping me on track and helping me maintain my sense of humor (or humour, in the case of my British cousins). I was often outgunned by their superior intellect and had to make appropriate adjustments to my commentary accordingly.

My colleagues at Adknowledge were particularly helpful in stimulating my imagination on one hand and forcing me to face reality on the other. My experience there reinforced my long-held belief that the most powerful people are those who have both the vision to see new opportunities and the technical know-how to exploit those opportunities in a timely and effective manner. I learned a great deal from the dynamic leadership of Adknowledge's founder Scott Lynn.

Most of all I am grateful to my wife, Jan, who gave up her position as assistant managing editor of the *South Bend Tribune* to follow me in retirement to Kansas City and, ultimately, use her editorial skills to help improve my writing. We share a great respect for the power of the written word and the publish-or-perish mandate.

INDEX

ABOUT THE AUTHOR

Lawrence C. Marsh is professor emeritus in the Department of Economics at the University of Notre Dame (http://sites.nd.edu/lawrence-c-marsh/home/). He taught graduate and undergraduate economics at Notre Dame for 30 years beginning in 1975. In 1990 he cofounded the Midwest Econometrics Group, which he directed for 15 years (http://www.nd.edu/~meg). He served as Director of Notre Dame's PhD program in economics for 13 years. He served in 2010 as visiting professor of econometrics and statistics in the MBA program at the University of Chicago's Booth School of Business and in 2016–2017 at Avila University in statistics and research methods in psychology.

He has also worked in business operations and management in the Aerospace Industry and for an internet advertising and online auction company. He has contributed to the *Kansas City Star* online edition as an independent *Midwest Voices* columnist. After serving in the U.S. Army in Vietnam, he returned home to take a job with Bendix Corporation's Aerospace Division as subcontract administrator and contract personnel administrator on the Apollo Moon Landings Mission, the Earth Resources Technology Satellite and a number of classified military projects. He worked at the internet advertising company Adknowledge, Inc. where he served as the head of analytics for banner targeting and as "statistical design strategist" in devising algorithms that send billions of banner ads to websites all over the internet. He has contributed to hundreds of publications including articles in the *Journal of Econometrics, Marketing Science, Statistics in Medicine,* and many other professional journals as well as numerous newspaper columns, book chapters, and books.

In teaching he won the James A. Burns award for excellence in graduate teaching in 1990–1991 and was an O'Malley Award Nominee for undergraduate teaching in 1995–1996. In 2002–2003 he was selected as a Kaneb Faculty Teaching Fellow for excellence in teaching. He has served on 80 PhD dissertation committees and has given several thousand lectures in graduate and undergraduate statistics, econometrics, mathematical economics, microeconomic theory, and research methods in psychology. In quasi-retirement he spends his time writing and editing a variety of articles, books, and newspaper columns.